Advance praise for E

"This is a brave, beautifully written account of Molly Best Tinsley's parents' final years in America's new solution—the continuing care facility. She shows us that no matter where we decline and
finally die, it is both tragedy and triumph."

Shannon Ravenel, editor, *New Stories from the South*

"While Molly Best Tinsley's story of her parents' last years is the
dark end of the family romance, you discover the dignity and un-
expected comedy of their struggle. It also charts the journey of
three siblings from denial to indignation and finally acceptance
as they learn how to bring comfort to a mother and father who
inhabit their own inner worlds."

Merrill Leffler, editor, Dryad Press; poet, *Mark the Music*

"Luminous, funny, and heartbreaking, *Entering the Blue Stone* is
a beautiful book—the writing, of course, but also the quality of
heart—it is so informed by love, without being in the least senti-
mental."

Joyce Reiser Kornblatt, *The Reason for Wings*

"What happens when one's larger-than-life military parents--so
strong, so capable, so valiant--begin to slide out of control? Molly
Best Tinsley tells the story of her parents' final battle--roles are
reversed, rules are unclear, and the entire family is engulfed by a
strange and deepening fog. It is a story both familiar and exceed-
ingly rare, beautiful and harrowing and often very funny. *Entering
the Blue Stone* is a small gem of a book. Read it."

Mary Edwards Wertsch
Military Brats: Legacies of Childhood Inside the Fortress"

Entering the Blue Stone is a necessary, compelling, beautifully crafted story. With tenderness and humor, Molly Best
Tinsley weaves lyrical childhood memories, medical details
of her parents' decline, and insights about the passing of life."

Geraldine Connolly, poet, *Hand of the Wind*

Entering the Blue Stone

A FAMILY. A PASSAGE. A MEMOIR.

Also by Molly Best Tinsley

fiction

My Life with Darwin
Throwing Knives: Stories
Satan's Chamber
(with Karetta Hubbard)

non-fiction

The Creative Process
(with Carol Burke)

Novelist, playwright, and the U.S. Naval
Academy's first *professor emerita,*
Molly lives in Ashland, Oregon.

Entering the Blue Stone

A FAMILY. A PASSAGE. A MEMOIR.

Molly Best Tinsley

FUZE
PUBLISHING LLC.
McLean, Virginia

Fuze Publishing LLC

1350 Beverly Road, Suite 115-162
McLean, VA 22101

P.O. Box 3128
Ashland, OR 97520

Book design by Ray Rhamey

ISBN 978-0-9849908-1-8
Library of Congress Control Number: 9780984990818

Dedication

For Cathy and Chris,
and in memory of Billy

❧ PROLOGUE ❧

Remember this.

The Jersey shore in the fifties: a woman in a shirred, boned, skirted one-piece poses high on the beach under an umbrella, her mouth fixed in a half-smile, her brow pinched. The baby she is carrying has not yet started to show. The morning sickness it causes lasts all day.

A scrawny boy in bouffant swim trunks shivers in the foreground. His father hollers to him, dares him to get his feet wet—his two older sisters are already up to their knees—but he's a scaredy-cat. He shies from the challenge and scampers back up the sand.

The sisters each lunge for one of their father's pale, lotion-slick arms and let him drag them through the cold breakers, which smash across their thighs and bellies. The water rises to their chests, their necks, lifts them off the bottom then sets them down again.

They keep their heads tipped back when the water deepens because they don't want it to cover their faces. They are not scaredy-cats. On the swim team at home, they practice racing dives and put their faces in the water all the time to do the crawl. But this water is different, the way it pushes you around. It's a thick greenish-brown, so salty it burns your throat.

When the water goes shallow, they scan the approaching waves, spot the one behind the next that is starting to look mean. Its bulge has already sharpened to a crest spitting bubbles. *Here comes a big one*, they yell on cue. It swells higher, higher, until it towers over them.

Their father, for whom there is always one right way to do anything, from washing yourself in the bathtub to peeling an orange to assembling and flying a kite—their father has taught them what comes next. Threatened by a big one, it does no good to try to run back to shore. You will be going against the undertow, it will lock you in place while the sand slips out from beneath your feet and the force of the wave breaks right on top of you, uses you to mop the ocean floor.

No, when you see a big one coming, you have to give up on keeping your face dry and dive right into it. Their father shouts *Now*, and the three of them plunge head first through the terror, the turbulence. When they surface, it's in quieter water, their feet dropping back onto solid sand as if nothing had happened, though behind them the greenish-brown surge implodes in churning froth.

~ 1 ~

SECURITY SYSTEMS

Our parents were being robbed. They were missing big things like fifty-dollar bills, the 18K gold pendant that used to belong to our grandmother, Dad's favorite camera, credit cards. They were missing little things, gloves, flashlights, loose change. They were suffering embarrassment when they tried to pay for purchases in check-out lines. They were picking frantic arguments at home.

They suspected the teen-aged son of the mailman, whom they paid to do yard work, a beautiful boy, they said—just like my brother Chris when he was a child—but one of those, like my brother Bill, who knew how to charm and take advantage. There were also rumors of break-ins in town.

Their world had become uncertain, unsafe. What a coincidence—a miracle almost—when the telemarketer called to tout his expensive security system. It was an answer, and they'd always believed difficult predicaments yielded to answers. Cheaters never won, hard work paid off, love conquered but never hurt. And if you put your mind to it, for every problem, you could find a fix.

I could tell their hopes had leaped beyond misplaced carkeys. This complicated system of alarms might finally restore order and serenity to their lives.

"I got tired of her worrying about East St. Louis moving in on us," Dad told me over the phone. Now if someone tried to enter the locked house, a siren would shriek. Somehow it could also sense alien body heat or footsteps around the perimeter when our parents were at home, and send out another alert. Then there was the button in their coat closet, which one of them could push in case of emergency. "If your father falls," Mother chimed in, "how would I stand him up again?"

Whatever the calamity, the system was going to signal a central switchboard in New Jersey. Then the monitor in New Jersey would notify the three-man police department back in our parents' town in southern Illinois, as well as the family member our parents had designated.

Fine. Where was the harm? It was their money. If it kept them busy, gave them comfort, what more could you ask? Besides, I wasn't the family member they decided to designate. Although my sister Cathy lived in northern Virginia, she was a lawyer, and since security systems reinforced the law, they'd reasoned that she should be the chosen one.

Soon she was being contacted a couple times a week, sometimes in the middle of the night, by a telephone voice with a Jersey accent announcing unspecified trouble a thousand miles away.

When she dialed our parents' number, she found them in a state of high excitement over the surprise visit just paid them by the Chief of Police. Still too distracted by the honor of it, they couldn't really pay attention when she tried one more time to talk them through the procedures for unlocking their front door or to warn them about that button in their closet—*for emergencies only: otherwise, do not touch.* "Remember the boy who cried wolf," she'd say. Our father had invoked that fable enough times when we were kids. "After a while, nobody's going to pay any attention."

To me my sister said, "We'd better start thinking about what to do with them." Meanwhile she took on ATT to see if we could get the system removed and at least some of their thousands of dollars back.

I couldn't imagine what she meant—*do with them*—other than what I'd always done, which was pick up the telephone once a week and listen to the latest griefs and grievances: brother Bill's dive from bipolar disorder into addiction, all our divorces, our father's frustrations with local politics, his eroding health.

"What did we do wrong?" they always got around to asking, and in terms too elaborate and theoretical to hurt feelings, I would try to explain. Smug in my enlightenment after years of psychotherapy, I thought I knew.

"You act like they used to be normal," I told my sister. "They'll get by. They always do."

They weren't that old by today's standards, not even seventy. The world was full of AARP poster couples, playing golf and tennis, strolling hand in hand through grocery stores, waiting for tables in restaurants, dozing at the symphony— some of them must have also had have security systems they couldn't quite master.

"What about the car?" Cathy asked. Our father had just had a minor accident. He'd grazed a bridge support in the LTD. "What if next time it's a station wagon full of kids? How are you going to feel then?"

She had me there. Dad pulled into traffic with something to prove: Brigadier General, USAF, retired; former mayor of Lebanon, Illinois. Bill Best was a man of importance, authority. The world would have to rearrange itself if he wanted to change lanes. "I just put on my turn-signal," he'd often told me, "and go."

৵৶

He stands on a parade ground, reviewing block after block of blue uniforms filing past. The band is playing "Wild Blue Yonder," flags are flapping, salutes jerk in robotic unison. He is at his official peak.

As the new commander of Air Weather Service, he is making his snippet of history. From the grandstand draped in red, white, and blue, my sister and I try to keep our squirming children in their seats, convinced that once out of sight the marchers are double-timing back to the starting line for another round.

The brim of his hat shadows the upper half of his face. The lower half isn't smiling. His chin juts forward as befits this occasion of high seriousness. It is a time to show uncompromising strength. A time if there ever was one when the code we have lived by applies: *feelings under wraps and mouths shut outside the family.*

It wasn't that we had terrible secrets to hide, just that the world was not a friendly place. Outside the family fortress, you needed to be perfect, invincible, to put your *best* foot forward. Forget love; it was respect you were after, edged with intimidation. You wouldn't dream of mentioning depression, collapsing marriages, a fondness for vodka or pot. Actually we never mentioned these things inside the fortress either, not until they stared us right in the face.

At work our father chewed his nails down to barely visible dents on the ends of his fingers. At home, he slathered baby cream on them and encased them in an old pair of leather gloves. To get to sleep, he wrapped his head in a special blanket, which our mother replaced every few years because he had to fiddle with its satin binding all night, eventually wearing it away.

He was tall but not muscular, with long, straight legs. He liked to tell us that our mother had the brains in the family; she'd retort that he had the legs. According to her, he was *fine-boned*, a fact she'd mention in order to emphasize her own *large* bones, something you actually wanted to have when you were checking one of those charts that dictated your ideal body weight.

Being musical, our father could dance, but he was no athlete. For years I blushed for him whenever he dove into a swimming pool: his stroke was stiff, tentative, and he didn't cup his hands.

As The Boss in the family, he had us children all figured out. I was the Sarah Bernhardt. Cathy sulked, then turned into Miss Sunshine the minute she was out of the house. Bill was temperamental and lacked common sense, but Chris you could strand in the wilderness and he would survive eating berries and newts.

He coached us with our schoolwork, and assigned us hobbies according to our talents and inclinations as he perceived them. If I liked to ice skate, my sister would be encouraged to ski. If she collected coins, I was to take an interest in stamps. He chose our colleges, and wrote the essays that accompanied our applications, inscribing them with his own grandiose dreams. Mine outlined plans to pursue medical research—which was why I had to take Latin in high school, so as to have an easy time later with the scientific names of body parts and germs.

"If only I'd had some guidance when I was a kid," he used to say.

We never heard the end of that.

I told him over the phone not to pick me up at the airport. I didn't want to put him to any trouble, I said, meaning I didn't want someone scraping me off a bridge support.

I rented a two-door Geo for the weekend, and pulling out onto the highway, I whacked one of those white and orange roadwork barrels, shattering the mirror on the driver's side.

The chrysanthemums had exploded gloriously along the flagstone path to their front door, upstaging the untended rest of the garden—withered coneflowers, coreopsis, daisies, and phlox—clogged with weeds. Before my raised fist could make contact with their door, it swung open, and there they were, buttoned into their L. L. Bean jackets, hats in their hands.

"We thought your plane crashed," Mother said, her lipstick fresh and fiery and not precisely on her mouth.

"We thought you could take us to Sylvie's for lunch," said Dad, as if I'd just dropped in from down the street. His white hair was combed crisp, but he strained to hold his head up, his chin fell slack, his shoulders sagged, and his eyes looked huge and glassy behind thick lenses.

"Wait till you taste her Reuben," said Mother.

They stood patiently on the front stoop while I stashed my suitcase and went to the bathroom.

"I'll take the backseat," Dad announced once we were outside. He opened the front passenger door. I looked at the sliver of space between the front seat and the door jamb.

"Are you sure you can squeeze through there?" I asked.

He pushed forward the front seat, looking determined, a camel facing the needle's eye. "This way you and Mommy can talk," he said.

"You might have trouble getting out," I said.

He staggered backward, shrugged. "I thought you two needed to talk."

"Well, it's only three blocks," I said.

At that, Mommy, who seemed to have shrunk since I saw her last, slipped through the V-shaped opening like Houdini. It was fairly easy on the other end to grab her hands and drag her out.

When she took off her jacket in Sylvie's Café, I was surprised to see her mother's gold pendant on its heavy chain around her neck. I lifted it in my palm. "Hey, great, you found this," I said. "So where was it?"

"I think that boy must have brought it back," she said.

"She wants me to fire him anyway," Dad said. "She gets me to do all the dirty work."

"Your father ran over a cat," she told me. "It came darting out of nowhere, and he put on the gas."

"That is not a true statement," he told me. Our eyes met. His were full of questions—did I believe him, did I see what he was putting up with?

I smiled and let my gaze slip away.

"I don't like to cook anymore," she confessed as we began to eat our grilled sandwiches.

"A brand new stove and Mommy doesn't even use it. I'm living on cereal and peanut butter."

"Actually grains and nuts make as good a protein as meat," I said.

As mayor, he'd fought the forces of anti-government conservatism to apply for and obtain a federal grant for a senior citizens' dining room. He personally delivered countless meals on wheels. But it would have been showing a dangerous weakness to pick up the phone and ask for help himself.

"When I think about food, I get butterflies," Mother said. "It makes me too sad."

The first night the new computerized stove almost defeated me. The instruction book was nowhere to be found, and it took a lot of trials and errors to get the thing to turn on. I fixed the meal which in the past our mother would have—lasagna and garlic bread. The aromas filled the house and lifted all our spirits, especially Dad's.

"Hey, Evvie," he sang as he sashayed stiffly into the kitchen, and made a stab at tickling her. "Do a little dance with goosey, goosey gander."

I set the table in the dining room, nicely with cloth napkins in pewter rings. I put the parmesan in its own pottery bowl, poured ice water into crystal glasses.

"Your father wouldn't know a sudden urge if it bit him," Mother confided when he had left us alone. "They just come over me and I want to move the sofa or put in all new roses or get on a bus heading south." As she complained, she gathered up the silverware I'd laid at each place. In two hands she bore the utensils back to the kitchen and slowly released them on the counter beside the sink. I felt a laugh welling up—the kind you cry at the end of. I'd been doing so well, being so neutral, impervious. I couldn't fall apart now. "Why don't we put these back at each place where they belong," I said.

"Of course," she answered.

I didn't check the table until it was time to sit down. Forks and knives lay in X's and V's down its center. The room hummed with a new, inscrutable code.

◈

The Noritake apple—larger than the real fruit, cast in two pieces, shiny red vessel and shiny red lid you lifted by a thin brown stem. Along with a silver coffee service, lacquer tables, prints framed in bamboo, and twelve place settings of Noritake dishes, our mother picked it up during our tour of duty in Japan after World War II, and its two halves had survived at least a dozen moves. In the beginning it held sugar cubes at informal dinner parties when the silver service might have been construed as showing off. Then little envelopes of fake sugar came along, and it dressed them up. Now as a prop in their denouement, it brimmed with pills: hormones, vitamins, our father's medications for Parkinson's disease, pills for depleted thyroids, pills for elevated blood pressure, pills for depressed souls. Every shape and shade of pill, all mixed together.

But Dad had this potentially confusing situation under control. He had created two legends on file cards, gluing a sample of each pill down the left margin and connecting it by dotted line to the dosage information on the right. He propped them between the salt and pepper shakers. The first morning of my visit, he and Mother studied the cards as if for the first time. Then with a strange sort of passion, they took turns fishing around in the apple, prolonging the tactile pleasure of all those precious chemical stones sifting through their fingers. That apple promised answers—for every problem, a fix.

Despite surgery twice for diverticulitis, a bad day still doubled Dad over with abdominal pain. Two operations on the veins of his legs had left his size eleven feet so sensitive that he shuffled around in size thirteen Rockports. Our mother suffered from headaches and rampant anxiety that a cornucopia of medication barely touched.

Ten years before, we'd searched out the name of a top psychiatrist in St. Louis for her. We needed a wise man, possessed of a compassionate ear and some insight that just kept eluding us.

"Depression has nothing to do with life situation," he decreed. "It is the result of a chemical imbalance." The only way to correct it was with pills.

After a couple of months of them, Mother had phoned me. "My medicine's backing up on me," she'd said. "The doctor's going to change me to something else." Then the something else backed up on her. None of his *something else's* seemed to work. He played his last card—electroshock therapy—calling it the ace up his sleeve.

We children protested, pleaded for a second opinion. But here again was a pat answer. Dad urged her on. When she came home from the hospital afterwards, I stayed with her for a week, and over mugs of coffee at the kitchen table, we tried to reprise the gossipy analysis we used to fall into of family members and friends. She had trouble remembering

names. Between platitudes and *non sequiturs*, her hand wandered toward a cluster of bottles in the middle of the table.
Some pills lay loose among them. Her fingers went for them
reflexively, pinched them up, had lifted them to her mouth
before I could stop her.

"You can't do that," I scolded. "You can't just take any old
pill any old time."

Now ten years later, our parents moped and sometimes
raged at their failure to be fixed, yet they still believed in the
possibility of fixing. I could tell by the reverential way they
assembled their allotment of pills from the Noritake apple.

I grasped each of them by the arm. "You're sure now
you've got the right ones?"

Of course they were.

Dad took his one at a time in the order they appeared
on the file card. Mother got an extra kick out of amazing me
with her ability to swallow all hers in one gulp.

The next day I cooked and froze casseroles, banana bread,
beef stew. I dictated instructions to Dad on how to defrost
each dish, and he wrote every step down on a pad on his
clipboard—underneath the page that reminded him how to
set the VCR to tape old movies from TV. He was upbeat, in
his element, nailing down a difficult procedure in written
steps. And I was *stocking their larder*: the phrase cheered him
as much as the fact.

Inspired by an influx of hope, he realized that what he
and Mother needed was one place in the house where they
could put anything of importance they had to be able to find

quickly—keys, receipts, gloves, my mother's purse, the flash-light, Clorets, instructions on working the stove. *A hoddy hole*, he called it.

He proposed the top drawer of an antique cabinet in the hall, where some important things already were, and we set about emptying it of things that didn't qualify, like old cough drops, candle stumps, wads of bent photographs, a balled up pair of pantyhose.

We were getting organized. They both vowed *no more frantic searches*. They would honor the principle of the *hoddy hole*. Make the extra effort to return things to it.

To top it off the next day, a man came out to disconnect the external alarm system. Dad could turn the key in his own door again without bringing on sirens, long distant phone calls, curious neighbors, patient police. Now he could say, "East, west, home is *Best*," the way he used to, with Mother and us children bumping up behind him, and feel it was true.

It was the last evening of the visit, Mother had gone to bed early, leaving Dad and me to watch his tape of *The Glenn Miller Story*, a film I admitted I'd never seen. I understood right away why he enjoyed Jimmy Stewart in this role—he must have recognized his own mix of humility and plain-talking irreverence—but June Allyson as the tirelessly competent kewpie helpmate seemed a painful mockery of the bewildered woman upstairs.

Mr. and Mrs. Glenn Miller's true love was about to conquer all, their hard work just beginning to pay off, when Dad killed the volume to say, "You know, Mommy sleeps a lot."

I said maybe she needed to.

"She slept thirty-seven hours last week."

I pointed out that was less than six hours a night.

"In a row."

All at the same time? Was he sure that many? On the screen in a monolithic dirndl skirt and high heels, June Allyson tended a bundle of newborn joy.

"So what did *you* do for thirty-seven hours?" I asked.

"Sat in the rocker and waited for her to wake up."

My brain jammed. Were her sleep and his resignation accidents? Shouldn't we be trying to prevent another? What was he talking about? I was supposed to ask questions, draw the information out of him, pronounce an emergency, promise to take action. I just wanted to go home.

There was a stubborn edge to his nonchalance. It reminded me of my brother Bill in his twenties, opening his collar to show me rope burns on his neck. Or bragging about the bottle of sedatives he'd amassed which he kept on his person at all times, just in case. Had we come to that?

"What are you trying to tell me?" I asked.

He shrugged.

"Well, what do you want me to do?"

"Are you interested in watching any more of this?" he asked back, then clicked the screen dark. "He gets killed in the end."

"Could she have gotten hold of some sleeping pills?" I asked. "I didn't see a sleeping pill on those file cards."

"You should probably know that Mommy and I have

made a suicide pact," he said with an attempt at bravado, a last-ditch flourish.

I felt as if I'd caught them in an intimate act. *Please, cover your souls*, I wanted to say. Cathy would have called his bluff, asked what form the pact took, told him she would respect it, if that's what they'd decided. Chris would have cajoled him into denying serious intent.

All I could think was, *I can't be sucked in.* Tomorrow I could go home. "Are you saying it had something to do with that, her long sleep?"

He slumped in his chair, dropped his chin onto his chest. "How do I know?"

"Maybe you just lost track of the time."

"I can't get through to her. She's acting all on her own."

Thirty-seven hours. A measure of emptiness, a black hole I didn't want to go near. "Why didn't you push the button in the closet?" I snapped. "I think that's the sort of emergency it's there for."

The day I was leaving, they were scheduled to see Mother's latest psychiatrist, who had been prescribing antidepressants for them both. There was enough time before my flight that I could share their appointment and meet the doctor and his colleague in social work who gave each parent a half hour of talk therapy twice a month. I imagined we would all five sit down together and evaluate the situation. I knew I should mention what our father had told me the night before.

Since I was going to the airport right from the doctor's, we took separate cars. Dad drove the LTD with its scraped fender, and I followed behind, a very slow micro-caravan of missed turns, doubling back, passing by the two-story, dingy brick storefront once, then going all the way around the block before pulling up in front. It was the sort of building where you'd expect loan companies and vacuum cleaner repair shops—a suite of frosted glass and crisp carpet, with a leggy philodendron on a Danish modern table, chairs with sagging seats, and the odor of wet wool.

I'd hated Mother's well-reputed psychiatrist at Barnes Hospital, his height and pleasant blandness, the obligatory navy blazer and grey slacks, his calm, barely inflected voice, his made-up mind: when his drugs then his plugs failed to work on her, it was somehow her fault.

Now here was her punishment, in a suit out of the seventies with wide lapels and flared trousers and a toupee. It was so shiny and black, it lowered his forehead so drastically—what could he be thinking? I gave him the benefit of the doubt, myself the benefit of a fantasy: maybe what we had here was a simple man, unpretentious and truly wise, whose top of the head was sensitive to cold, and who just didn't care what people thought. I was already on that flight to IAD. Getting cleared for departure.

He was the first of a number of doctors I would hear yell at our mother, assuming, I supposed, that all old people are deaf. His question was simply, "How are you today?" but I saw her flinch, put up her front, the way she did when Dad raised his voice and she was resolving to do whatever she had to do, say whatever she had to say, to get him to lower it.

"I think, better," she said softly and he gave her cheek a couple hard pats.

"Had any more of those headaches?"

"Maybe a few. They weren't so bad. I took some Tylenol."

This was what he wanted to hear. Now, did I have any questions?

"What might make my mother sleep for thirty-seven hours in a row?" I asked. He didn't want to hear that anymore than I did.

"Well, it all depends," he said. "When exactly did you see her sleep that long?"

"I didn't. My father told me."

"Oh, your father," he said, with a glance toward Mother that said *We shouldn't talk about these things around her.* Then he began yelling again. "So, Mrs. Best, you've been feeling a little tired lately?" A nod from her. "How about if you mention that to Mr. Anderson when you see him?"

When it was Dad's turn, the doctor approached him with the same loud cheeriness, but Dad would never have said that he was fine, Dad was always terrible. He got angry with Mother if she answered a casual inquiry into their health too automatically, without painting the extent of his misery. He claimed that he wanted people to know all about it so they wouldn't expect anything of him anymore. He said he wanted to be left alone. He was polishing the last chapter in the story of his life—a man dedicated to public service, elected mayor by a landslide, who had to step down in the middle of his second term because the obstinate stupidity of his enemies broke his health. Now half-crippled with Parkinson's disease and chronic pain, he was the brigadier general of suffering, the mayor of unjust fate.

We still had to get through the half hour with the caring Mr. Anderson, in his shirtsleeves, argyle vest, and scuffed shoes. He had plenty of real hair and down-to-earth cowlicks and faith in positive thinking.

Were they stopping to smell the roses? he wanted to know. Were they turning off sad memories? Were they giving each other and themselves little treats? *Yes*, they said. *Yes.* They seemed pleased. The correct answer was more important than an accurate one.

The performance continued. Who was responsible for Bill's health? Not Evelyn. Who was responsible for Evelyn's sorrow? Not Bill. Mother agreed to think better of herself, then shed some obliging tears.

"Who is the one person in charge of your happiness?" Mr. Anderson asked her. That was a difficult one. Was she considering the expert over at Barnes, or his Medicare-bred version in the next room? Or was she tempted to try to explain how entangled our father's being was with her own? "It's yourself, isn't it, Mrs. Best?" coached Mr. Anderson. Mother conceded another *yes*.

Dad agreed to listen more tolerantly to Mother's feelings, then tried to explain his new concept of the hoddy hole. Mr. Anderson moved the discussion to the value of making lists. Finally Dad confessed, "We tend to wait a little long or cut a little short and then it all goes kerflooey."

By the time I brought up the question of Mother's thirty-seven-hour sleep, it seemed irrelevant at best, at worst, perverse, an attempt to spoil the pleasant mood that had filled in the cracks in the room. Mr. Anderson said something tactful and caring and jotted down the information. I considered asking him if he knew anything about a suicide pact, but then decided that would also be perverse. I decided I shouldn't be such a snob. Unfashionable clothing did not brand a person incapable of helping an elderly couple. They didn't need a superhuman intervention. They just needed mottoes enough to make it through each day.

I put away the thought that our mother might have been trying to die, that our father might have been willing to let her. When I reported the incident to Cathy and Chris, it had lost much of its solidity even as a probable accident.

I put away the fact that our parents *were* dying, and with them would go parts of ourselves. I put away all the doubts that start clamoring as life withers and the layers peel away from its vacant heart. I boarded my flight back to Washington, DC, with the same deep breath, the same righteous relief I'd always felt after a visit—*well, that's out of the way for a while.*

In less than a month, our mother would have to be hospitalized for seeing prostitutes with white-painted faces and cats chewing up the bedclothes and defecating in her food. She would claim not to know our father, and, hurt and confused to the core, he would begin to refer to her as *somebody,* as in "Somebody doesn't want to have anything to do with me anymore," or as *him*, as in "We're having him watched," or even, inexplicably, as *Max*, as in "You can tell from the pictures that Max is dead."

After dozens of impossible phone calls, Chris and Cathy would take turns flying out to St. Louis. Finally Chris would arrange to have them airlifted to an Air Force base in North Carolina, where he would pick them up and drive them the four hours to his home in Durham, where they could be tested by doctors he was familiar with, our mother's drugs could be monitored, the antidepressants she'd been popping at whim could be cut back, and our father could get some rest.

Cathy and I would come down to help with their various medical appointments, after which she and I would transport them to her house in Virginia for several weeks, while Chris and I flew back to Illinois to pack up their house and get it on the market. At the same time we would put in their application to a new facility in Durham for something called *continuing life care*. We were executing plans as fast as we could devise them.

Cathy was driving the four of us toward Virginia, Dad in the shotgun seat, when he attempted clarity: "I'm going to tell you now because I always forget: Mommy has two sicknesses and I have one other diagnosis. Mommy's is Alzheimer's and the other is what, sweetie?" When Mother didn't answer but stared resolutely out her back window, our father and commanding officer tried to rally us. "We're going to lick this all by standing together," he said in a thin voice. "The only difficulty is, am I here and is Mommy there?"

⌐~ 2 ~⌐

A HISTORY OF HOME

We had the weekend to pack up their home.

Chris and I flew into St. Louis with a box of trash bags in my suitcase and hit the ground running—upstairs to the bedrooms, down to the basement, flinging open closets, cabinets, emptying shelves, dumping drawers, in a controlled frenzy of deconstruction.

I tackled Mother's walk-in closet, stuffed with tweed and plaid, knife-pleated skirts, tailored blazers, woolen sweaters dyed to match, paisley blouses with neck bows. She'd clung to the Peck and Peck look long after Peck and Peck went out of business and discount chains sold its sturdy classicism off-price. It was her uniform, which she'd earned the right to wear, having graduated from a Seven Sisters college *Phi Beta Kappa*, after majoring in philosophy and writing her senior thesis on the subject of angels.

Philosophy, when her brain danced to a logic all its own? When she couldn't balance a checkbook, and never managed to drive a car smoothly, not having any idea of the connection between the hocus pocus her feet and hands had memorized and the mechanics of an automobile?

She tended with large numbers to be off by some factor of ten. Serving company, she dished out one too many plates of food, or poured one drink too few. The rest of us played word games, card games, board games, but she hardly ever joined in, because she found the rules arbitrary and unreasonable. If she did play, she forgot them, ignored them, broke them, then told us we weren't being nice when we took her to task.

And *angels*, when she loathed her father's Catholicism, and by extension, any *fol de rol* that smelled of religion? She said she believed in "a boundless divine light, and we're all part of it, each a flicker." Unlike me, who started early, cramming my kid's brain with phobias, from car crashes to quicksand, lockjaw to leukemia, she'd never been afraid of death. Quite the contrary. It intrigued her like the fantasy of a romantic affair.

She did use the word *spiritual* a lot, often to point out a serious deficiency of mine. She had zero sympathy for my dogged efforts as an adolescent to scrape together enough of the right clothes to avoid being ostracized in one new school after another.

This ongoing enterprise marked me as a *materialist*, a *clotheshorse,* a shallow, unworthy person. Better to pay attention to *spiritual* values, put your faith in that which lasts.

I reciprocated her scorn. A generation later she might have been a flower child, later still a New Ager, but in the fifties she cramped my style. It wasn't just no lipstick, no short shorts, no padded bras. It wasn't just being forced to read *Wuthering Heights* and *The Mill on the Floss* when all I wanted was to be friends with Sandra Dee.

She scoffed at Christmas and other holidays as commercial scams. She got furious if I mindlessly sang some advertising jingle that had snagged in my brain.

She went on to deride clothing emblazoned with logos or designers' names. Only idiots turned their bodies into billboards. When a salesperson told her to *have a nice day*, she'd turn to me and explain loudly, "She's just saying that so you'll buy more."

But if one minute she was criticizing me for wanting to wear what everyone else wore, talk the way everyone else talked, the next she'd hold up *what people might think* as a sacred standard. She was a nonconformist who feared disgrace.

The mountain of clothes heaped on her bed blared this hypocrisy, or irony, at least. All that material indulgence, redolent of moth balls and Replique perfume, garments enough for half-a-dozen wardrobes. And they were certain to last longer than the woman stashed at Cathy's house in Virginia, tangling night and day into a skein of emergencies. She was seeing cats everywhere, calling our father a stranger, couldn't remember that she'd been given *her* Tylenol less than an hour ago, two hours ago, three, and couldn't stop emptying out the dresser drawers.

Our mother, stripped of disguises like refinement, intelligence, self-denial—her spirit vanishing before our eyes.

ॐ

Their bond was what we knew of earthly permanence. Fifty years as soul-mates, soul-enemies, two living as one. Fifty years of remaking the same home in different apartments and houses. As Chris and I packed and sorted and trashed, we told each other, "Look at the good side—it's not like we ever lived here." We never lived very long in any house as kids. Maybe all that packing up and snapping of attachments, all those dry good-byes, had been toughening us for this.

This house was supposed to have sheltered their *golden years*, a comfortable nest cluttered with the stuff they'd collected in their travels, a twenty-minute drive from the commissary, BX, and hospital on Scott Air Force Base. Mother was supposed to spend her days puttering around in the attached greenhouse, while Dad pored over his finances at his huge oak desk. They were supposed to keep a close eye on the Weather Channel and tape more three-star old movies than they could ever watch, and rock themselves into a final, painless sleep on the side porch.

It's all history now, not even History—just the debris of a *family of origin*, swimming in memory's haze.

Like those photographs. They drove Chris and me to the brink, finding them stashed by the hundreds everywhere, in folders, shoeboxes, or loose clumps. One of us opened the drawer of the credenza in the dining room, or the telephone table, or a nightstand, and a compressed stack of them began to rise—warped, cracked, faded faces, in our face. "Guess what I just found?" we took turns calling out. Soon neither of us bothered to chime the answer: "More pictures."

Our father was an accountant at heart. He'd always kept a daily record in the same grey loose-leaf notebook of every penny he and Mother had ever spent or saved. Photographs were another way of keeping track of what he had. Deposits in a fly-by-night bank: *open the album, read the story of my happy family, they're all here, saved, organized, saying cheese.*

It was during our tour in Japan that he got hooked on cameras, where I first remember his neck slung with them and their accessories. Japan gave birth to the home movie, endless footage of his wife and children opening doors—screen doors, car doors, school doors—then taking ordered steps in the direction of the camera, giving ordered waves. Soon he was shooting amateur travelogue—Buddhist temples and Shinto shrines, Sumo wrestlers, shoppers on the Ginza.

After we moved back to the States, the first week of school put big pressure on us kids. "Well?" he'd ask at the dinner table, meaning had we approached our new teachers yet on the subject of his Japanese movies? Eventually we'd make ourselves mention his willingness to come in and show them to the class. No teacher ever declined.

Early along he'd also learned how to splice the little reels into big ones, which streamlined his presentations. It meant that between coverage of the Emperor's Palace and a Boys'

Day parade, my classmates would be treated to the excitement of my sister and me in our good dresses and patent leather shoes, squeezing out the front door of our quarters and, dazed looks on our faces, waving from the stoop.

It still comes over me, the massive inertia whenever someone suggests lining up for a snapshot. Chronic camera fatigue, contracted in childhood. There we kids would be, rattling across Europe in our Chevy station wagon, reading comic books or singing to ourselves, given over to the suspended animation it took to survive a long car trip—*expeditios*, our father used to call them, in honor of Caesar. We'd feel the car slow, veer off onto the shoulder, hear the driver's door open, the assault of fresh air. "Everyone out for a picture," came the order. Grumbling and whining, we assembled in front of the glacier or the vineyard gate or the village chapel and faked smiles.

Then with his fine nose for injury, our father would complain that no one ever thought to get him in any of the pictures. So one of us would have to be reminded what buttons to push, after which he set up the shot, pulling out his light meter, measuring distances, then finally stepping into its center. "Don't chop my head off," he'd warn. "Cheese."

Every time our father pressed open the shutter, he thought he closed a door on life's muddle, conquered it. He never figured out that control was only ever for a moment, after which life bounced back hard.

There were early shots of our mother, her eyelids drooping, her mouth pursed in knowing bemusement. Even with

a diapered toddler on one arm and a four-year-old clinging
to her thigh, she tried to look seductive, dreamy, for the man
behind the camera. Vaguely embarrassing, those images of
longing, like plot complications arising too late, when a story
was almost over.

I remembered her telling me that she and our father "had
chemistry." It was right before my wedding, after she'd asked
out of the blue about my fiancé, "Have you slept with him?"

The question provoked the nausea that mother-daughter
moments had always induced in me. "Yes," I admitted, then
waited for the backlash. She was never to be trusted, and I
was afraid her next question would be, "Do you love him?"
What if I told her the truth, that love was beside the point,
that I was getting married because at age nineteen I couldn't
think of anything else to do?

But she'd surprised me by sounding envious. "I used to
ache for your father." They too spent weeks apart at different
colleges, she becoming an expert on angels, he, majoring in
math. When they were together, she would have surrendered
to the chemistry anytime, but he stopped them. "He said
it would have made him feel terrible not to do everything
right." So they waited until after the wedding, a simple civil
ceremony with no photographs. It was wartime, and besides
that, it was the best her immigrant father could afford.

Afterwards, our father enlisted in the Army. The legend
holds that he checked a box marked *meteorology* because the
recruiter told him he'd be studying collisions between meteors and Earth. At Officer Candidate School, he had to live

in the barracks Monday through Friday. Saturday mornings
our mother waited at the gate for him to appear. Too often
he didn't. He'd been restricted for insubordination, and she'd
have to take the bus back to her rented room alone.

An old studio portrait of him in sepia tones always sat
on her dresser: his lips are tinted pink, his cheeks rosy and
smooth, and he looks so young he is almost pretty. He is
still adolescent thin. His military hat perches on his close-
cropped head like a wide bowl, and his collar shows room
to spare. The look on his face is aw-shucks bashful, as if he
suspects the camera might be able to guess that when they
allowed him out on Saturday nights, he let himself get carried away.

We had to throw most of the pictures away, the loose
ones stuffed into boxes, the albums whose pages crumbled
to the touch. What else could we do? Time was running out.

Books and records we donated to the local college. Most
of Mother's indestructible woolens went to Goodwill, along
with a mysterious stack of brand new men's long underwear.
Within an hour after we put out the word, neighbors had
carried off all her African violets, cyclamen, orchids, bego-
nias, and ferns.

With an air of noblesse oblige, we offered the contents of
our parents' liquor cabinet to the packers, a husband, wife,
and their two grown sons. The wife looked at me with great
pity then whispered that their religion prohibited drink.

But pictures by the cubic foot? Our flattened faded past disappeared into black plastic bags.

In a blur of glimpses, vaguely I noted that by the time the boys were born, our mother's sensual languor before the camera had hardened into exhaustion, impatience. In the background it might have been the State House in Stockholm or an animal house in who knew which zoo. Or she might have been basting a turkey or coming in from who knew which garden with tomatoes and peppers piled along the curve of her arm. But her smile began to say, *Hurry up and get this over with, for heaven's sake.*

And then it collapsed into *I'm sorry.* Why, because the beauty she once embodied for our father's camera was slipping away? Because she'd grown to hate parties and receptions—command performances—and all the weeks he had to spend away from home? Because our father was devoted, responsible, hard-working—doing *it* all for *her*—when she didn't want *it*, she wanted *him?*

I wanted to find just one picture of her that suggested a head-thrown-back defiance, as if to say, *what a silly thing beauty is anyway—I've got better things to do than win best supporting actress in your film.*

Instead, there they stood on our father's desk, her proudly holding his arm, him straight as a pillar in the formal uniform of a general officer. He has climbed as high as he, a boy who had hoped to study the fall of meteors, was going to go. She wears a long flowered skirt and a pink silk blouse, and looks more beautiful than ever, because the plastic surgeon at the base hospital had some idle time between accident victims and has removed the bump she never liked in her nose.

Ꮨ

I settled for this: brown-and-white, cracked like old porcelain, capturing summer on a mountain path in the Poconos. Sunlight sifts through a lacy canopy, dappling the shoulders and hair of the girl and boy whose long strides say *serious hike* even though they are holding hands.

She is not quite a woman, in baggy shorts and saddle shoes with dark curls spilling over her brow. He seems a long way from a man, in long pants, a shirt with short, flapping sleeves, hair shaved almost to the scalp along the sides, waves rippling on top.

You can't tell that he has bad skin, although it would become one of his governing memories of that time. If one of us kids ever fussed over a blemish, he'd say, "When I was your age, I looked like someone had thrown a bucket of manure in my face." But here he seems pleased, if a little nervous, as if he were getting away with something. Holding a pretty girl's hand? Plotting a kiss? Pretending for a moment that his cheeks and forehead are like hers, tanned and smooth?

How does she look? Feverishly happy, I'd say. Triumphant. She has been called a go-getter. You had to be when your father left a small farm in Spain for Ellis Island and never learned to speak English right, when he worked his way up to skilled labor at Otis Elevator in Yonkers, but couldn't resist the race track, so that Friday nights were often disasters of swallowed anger and tears, instead of food.

You had to get all A's, sell the most subscriptions, win essay contests and a full scholarship to Barnard.

You aimed high when you fell in love—a doctor's son, a family with its own vacation cottage, whereas you were there at that summer resort to babysit a spoiled brat named Beryl.

That's what this is, the girl is thinking. *Love.* Not just another fickle crush.

Of all the things she has gone and gotten, this is the best.

❧ 3 ❧

THE SLIPPERY SLOPE

All the way over we coached them. *Who's the president of the United States? How many dimes in a dollar?* The correct answers would confirm their status as capable human beings.

Meanwhile, a stream of simple but impossible questions swirled in the panic I was barely controlling. *How do you keep a cyclamen blooming? How did your parents meet? And what angels, Mother—why angels? What caused your own father's death so young, Dad? And what do you think about the threat of global warming? I can't believe I've never asked.* It was too late to find out such things; we would never know. Those systems were crashing, their information melting back into neuro-chemical soup.

Besides, we had to focus on the faceless doctor looming ahead. He would be seeking important facts: *what day of the week is it? What state are we in?*

Emergency, I thought, but we couldn't let that show.

Actually, it was North Carolina and early December, the day overcast and cold. Our parents had been flown east with nothing but the two suitcases Dad gathered his wits long enough to pack.

According to Mother, the lights were kept off during the flight to conceal the carousing and consuming of Chinese food on the part of the crew. Dad had never protested her report. He was lying low where she was concerned. If after fifty years of a symbiotic marriage she was casting him aside in favor of a stranger with a motorboat, coming to take her to New Orleans, then he would ignore her right back. Meanwhile he still railed against nursing homes and swore they would never move out of their house. We hadn't the heart to tell him they already had.

They'd teetered who knew how long on the brink of what Dad kept calling *the slippery slope*. Now the balance had shifted, and everything was tumbling—marriage, family, home—all the art and craft of a love we'd taken for granted. It made me think of those tar pits, whole complex species being sucked into oblivion.

Test results had not come back, we reminded each other. There was no proving Alzheimer's anyway except by autopsy. Besides, we weren't going to talk about it. We had to protect our mother. We didn't want that ever-ready, free-floating anxiety of hers zeroing in on something all too real and specific, all too worthy of fear: Peter finally coming face to snout with the wolf.

But of course she knew. That was the problem. She had
caught the glint of an eye or a tooth, glimpsed the dark tail
swishing among the trees, and decided not to cry out for
once, not even to our father, in order to avoid the shame of
a disease that had replaced cancer as unspeakable, the death
worse than death.

Over the last years, the burden of making excuses for
herself must have caused even more anxiety, and she kept
taking more of her pills to subdue it. Except that the more
pills she took, the wilder her mind got, so she had to take
more pills, until they blew it apart.

That was my theory, anyway.

Ten days in Chris's guest room without anti-depressants,
and she was still seeing cats doing odd things in odd places
and children tumbling out of air vents. But we could explain those apparitions. Weren't there at least a dozen *real*
cats slinking around Chris's property, and weren't Lucas and
Zoey, Chris's children, so small and quick you never knew
where they were going to turn up next?

What we couldn't explain, we objected to and corrected,
often enough that she started ending her strange accounts
with the concession, "That was my imagination working."
One night while everyone slept, she'd performed in a stage
version of *A Connecticut Yankee* opposite our missing brother
Bill. After getting through Yale by managing his manic-de-
pression with alcohol and any illegal drug he could get his
hands on, he'd been rehabbed three times and finally drifted
out of contact with all of us. Mother had been a little sur-

prised, she said, that he knew all his lines, then she smiled coyly and added, "I know, it was probably a dream."

Such insights of hers fueled our hopes, our taste for fairy tales. Maybe under the spell of all that medication the mother of *our* dreams was waiting to be set free. It was too sweet to resist, the story with the happy ending. Besides it was the version of reality that stood the best chance of getting our parents past the Evergreen medical interview that lay ahead.

Evergreen was a brand-new life care community, a brand-new concept at the time. Its glossy binder of information implied that if you did everything right, spared no expense, a headfirst plunge down the slippery slope could be transformed into a smooth coast downhill.

Once through the concrete pillars and past the bed of ornamental cabbage, the road did curve down a hill. On the higher ground to right and left were clusters of cottages for those residents who didn't mind a brisk walk each evening to the central dining room located in the three-story apartment building, which stretched along the hill's base. Under one wing of this building, the terrain dropped off sharply, allowing for two more floors below the ground in front. One, Spruce Center, contained single rooms for those individuals who came to need help with dressing and taking their medicine. The floor below that, dug out of the hill, housed Pine Center, the inevitable nursing home, last stop, its one side dug right into the earth.

Today we all know the drill: you have to buy an apartment upstairs and then you begin your descent. Today, we all know that architecture and new terminology can't restore clarity, strength, a zest for living. In the mid-nineties, my sister and brother and I were happy to pay many thousands of dollars for the promise that they might.

But first our parents had to qualify. Someone official had to determine that they could function independently in that controlled environment. As we helped them out of the car in the parking lot, we were not sure what that meant, *function*, but we were sure that our mother could not have Alzheimer's. Rather, if she did have the disease, she must not be perceived to have it.

It was a family secret. We were used to those. We were ready to blame much of our current situation on the chaos of our mother's pills, at the same time asserting that we'd finally brought them under control.

She hadn't eaten properly in a month, but she almost looked trim and tailored, you almost didn't notice that her plaid Pendleton skirt and navy blazer seemed to hang empty from her shoulders and hipbones. One hour earlier, I'd waged a mighty battle with her pantyhose, which she had gotten twisted into a topological nightmare, but now serenity reigned.

Our father had on a tweed jacket, grey trousers, and a striped tie. To mute the pain in his feet and calves, he was also wearing his trademark giant Rockports over thick socks. Except for the clownish disproportion, he looked distinguished, professorial, with his horn-rimmed glasses and full head of white hair.

"Just be natural," I said, meaning the opposite. If we wanted to pass for a normal, healthy family, we knew we'd have to pretend.

"Nobody's expecting you to hop around like sixty-year-olds," Cathy said, in her hand-knit sweater and sleek slacks. She wore her own forty-five years as if they were fifteen—she never changed, my younger sister, with the silky strawberry blond hair.

Mother's laughter came a split-second after everyone else's, but then it always had. Jokes involved a dislocation of logic you might not notice if yours had never run on track.

Chris had thrown on an old sports coat over his work shirt and jeans. He might have even trimmed back his curly hair. "I'm betting on you, Dad," he said, slapping our father gently on the back. "Evergreen doesn't have a chance."

As the five of us advanced toward a dark green awning, I realized this was the first time we'd all been together since Cathy graduated from law school thirteen years before. I didn't see which one reached for the other, but our parents were holding hands. All at once I felt giddy, buoyed, dandled by an old current that ran deeper than drugs and disease.

We were the Bests. We were smarter than most people. Maybe that was our central family secret, because we never bragged. We let our performances speak. We lived our father's clichés. We put our best foot forward, and if others failed to listen and appreciate, they were presumed to be bumps on logs or to have their heads up their you-know-whats. It would always be us against the world.

From that vantage point, our mother could block out her childhood poverty, her mother whose gossip buzzed with *she don't* and *I says*, her immigrant father who managed on broken English until he died. Our father could forget those Princeton classmates whose own fathers had lived long enough to see them graduate, and thus had given them better guidance. He wasn't proud of having drifted into the military, and those other guys always seemed to be making more impressive livings than he.

The double doors swung apart, sucking us into a vaulted lobby, carpeted and draped like a four-star hotel in forest green and mauve. It smelled like a new car. A flower arrangement the size of three children erupted from a platform at its center—an offering to the goddess of décor. Behind it, a wide semi-circular staircase straddled a fountain into which water spilled soothingly from three tiers of giant granite bowls.

Chris, Cathy, and I had toured this place weeks before. Now we craned to read our parents' reactions. Were they impressed? Didn't we tell them it would be nice? Better than nice, *grand*. Nothing like the *old folks' home* they had conjured, the drab, disinfected last resorts their own parents had died in. If anything was good enough for the Bests, certainly this was.

They tried to act pleased, but even in their confusion they understood what we were trying to forget. Nothing was going to make up for the loss of their 1930s Tudor with its stone fireplace, stained-glass windows, our mother's dream greenhouse added on, and a breakfast bay that overlooked a riot of garden, bird feeders, fruit trees.

"Just remember all the times they uprooted us," I whispered to Cathy behind their backs. "Don't fight the problem, quote, end quote." Then it had been our father showing us through our new home, touting the new air base, schools, neighborhood, country, whatever.

In Japan two live-in maids were supposed to sweeten a move our mother fought in vain, but she could never figure out what to do with them. In Florida he found a log cabin on a bay for us to live in, where we could swim even in winter. But it was too near a paper mill, the water was polluted, and after two months, Cathy and I had amoebic dysentery. In Sweden Cathy and I were enrolled in *L'Ecole Francaise*, though *Frere Jacques* was the extent of our French. In Germany our family of six was quartered in adjoining two-bedroom apartments. Cathy and I slept in one then scooted across the first-floor landing in our pajamas for breakfast.

It was always easiest for our father because every move was a step up and every step up, a candle lit to his father's ghost. Otherwise he kept his emotional attachments pared down to his wife and kids. He enjoyed his cameras, the piano once we had one, his jazz records, and briefly, a couple tanks of tropical fish. But the only material objects he couldn't live without were his Scripto mechanical pencils, his Clorets, his nail clippers, and those blankets with the right kind of binding to wrap around his head when he slept.

"The trouble with you, Evvie," he chided our mother, "you tend to personalize everything." Meaning she got too

involved in things, too attached. Which opened the channel
for unhappiness.

We knew it tore her heart to leave certain places. She kept
them alive, the settings of legends, in a wistful, throaty voice.
Their first house had been out in the sticks of Annandale,
Virginia, and our father jounced into the Pentagon everyday
on the bus. As a girl in Yonkers she had spaded a patch of
the vacant lot behind her sixth-floor, walk-up apartment and
grown corn on the cob. In Annandale she got right down to
planting vegetables, raising chickens, and hobnobbing with
farmers. Fifteen years later in Massachusetts, when our parents scraped together the down payment for The House on
Parker Street, it was the paradise of Annandale regained.

A white two-story clapboard on over an acre, The House
on Parker Street hid behind a giant blue spruce that spread its
graceful arms to block out the road. It looked out in back on
an apple tree and a vegetable garden with an established asparagus patch. Assigned to the Strategic Air Command, our
father worked in an underground site somewhere in the hills.
During an alert, he'd be gone long hours, practicing retali-
ation against a Soviet launch of nuclear missiles, any one of
which would have wiped out all New England. Meanwhile,
Mother was either in the garden, *head down, tail up*, as our
father used to say, or in the kitchen freezing the foods she
had grown. Our father built a coop for more chickens. All we
needed was a dairy cow and a design for a flag to be a nation
unto ourselves.

I left for college from that house, but by the time spring

semester was over, our father had been transferred to An-
drews Air Force Base outside Washington, DC, and I came
home to a treeless subdivision of split-levels, block after block
of identically plotted front yards, and nothing out back but a
patio, with a view of other patios aligned in infinite regress.
Nowhere was there a ripening tomato or a frond of asparagus
going to seed.

We told ourselves then what we told ourselves now.

Don't push the panic button.

Don't fight the problem.

Put your best foot forward.

Take things in stride.

Maybe Dad's tapes were playing in Mother's head, because she put on the face she used to wear when she had
to attend some official function of the Officers' Wives, and
marched right over to a woman standing just inside the door,
probably waiting for a ride.

"Don't I know you?" she asked most cordially. "I'm Evelyn Best, and I believe we met at a coffee at June Seaver's."

If the woman thought the question strange, she didn't
show it. She could have been an officer's wife, I thought, with
her perfect teal blue suit and crisp hair and poised demurral.
The grey-haired couple studying the activity book in another
corner looked up and flashed us bright smiles.

I should have been feeling welcomed by them, reassured.
But something bothered me.

Was it the woman's silk warm-up, the man's V-neck
sweater with some emblem over the right breast? Their

matching pristine walking shoes? Why shouldn't the elderly be well-groomed? Still, I began to wonder. Maybe we should have found our parents a life care *farm*. Somewhere there must be such a place—I may need one soon myself—where an old woman can slip on a shift, stick her feet into rubber boots, and clomp out to a chicken yard to gather eggs and scatter corn.

We asked the woman by the door where the Wellness Clinic was then whisked Mother down the corridor in that direction. She cocked her head back toward the couple trying to decide which to sign up for—a theatre trip or a lecture on Africa.

"I know those people," she said. "They've been trying for such a long time to have a normal child."

In the clinic waiting room, there was one woman already sitting prim and permed when the five of us squeezed through the door. After some earnest smiling and introducing, we filled the silence with a prolonged fuss over who would stand and who would sit and where.

"Dad, you can sit in my lap," Chris suggested. "And then Mom can climb onto yours."

Cathy and I demonstrated that we could almost wedge ourselves both into one captain's chair. We joked about going on diets.

"Remember Crisco," Dad warned with a droll grin. "Fat in the can."

The woman crossed her legs in the other direction.

Well, better a relaxed vulgarity, I thought, than performance anxiety, or any other kind of anxiety Mother might be percolating.

The wait continued and our collective mood drooped. We couldn't keep up the banter. Despite its hopeful name, that clinic was just another doctor's office, like all the other doctor's offices where our parents had sat and waited to little avail. Maybe too we caught a glimpse of the truth, that we weren't really facing a showdown between The Best Brigade and the forces of numskullery, but merely a swag of red tape that was going to snap anyway. The apartment our parents had applied for was the largest model, most expensive and least popular. Marketing would have just as soon had it sold.

I noticed Mother appraising the other woman's patterned sweater, then before I could think of something to distract her, she introduced herself again and asked, "Isn't this a lovely room?"

There was absolutely nothing to distinguish the room except that it was so small that if one person moved, everyone else had to shift too. But the woman didn't seem to find the question odd. She agreed, and it bothered me, because you could almost hear under her courteousness the hum of tensed nerves. Maybe this woman was also waiting for some sort of official test. Maybe her future hinged on something she had to prove, or on something she had to hide—a brain that had begun to play tricks on her, a brain she couldn't quite trust anymore. Like someone who laughed at odd moments because she wanted to appear to get whatever joke might have just been cracked, she was prepared to agree with anything.

I braced for Mother to start in on one of her dreams, but she didn't. Instead she asked how long the woman had been living at Evergreen and whether she liked it.

"Oh yes, especially the food," the woman gushed, grateful for such an easy question. "Some of the recipes they take right out of *Gourmet Magazine*." As advertised. The woman had gained ten pounds in the three months since she had moved in.

"It certainly doesn't show," Mother said.

The woman pulled at the waistband of her skirt. "Pretty soon I'm going to need a whole new wardrobe."

"You must have been skin and bones before"

Cathy widened her eyes at me. I nodded. What could be more normal than that little woman-to-woman exchange? Too bad no one official was around to hear.

৵৵

Our father's story was sad and incontrovertible. His succession of diseases had been well-documented: diverticulitis, ruptured disc, bad gall bladder, phlebitis, prostate cancer, and finally Parkinson's—all physical, all clearly labeled in the medical books along with protocols and prognoses. Everything that could be done to cure or alleviate symptoms had been done.

With a sturdier helpmate, he might have been able to putter along independently for years, keeping incontinence just at bay, grappling with knife and fork, growing more and more quiet to avoid the forever it took to finish a sentence.

Could our mother be that sturdier helpmate? Nobody really knew at that point. Test results weren't back yet; everything was up in the air. When a man opened the door to the inner examining rooms and called her name, Mother flinched almost guiltily.

She knew. She was going to have to pass one more time for someone she didn't think she was, prove one more time she wasn't herself. Hadn't she been doing that all her life?

Cathy and I each took an arm and the three of us followed the young bearded doctor with basset-hound eyes and bouncy, thick-soled shoes. Mother began to tremble and breathe audibly. "I don't want to see a doctor right now," she whispered. "Why don't we go home now?"

Home. A slip of the tongue. We kept moving her forward, murmuring empty reassurances. She held her shoulders high and stiff.

The doctor talked a little too loud at her, patted her a little too hard and perfunctorily, as if to prove he could do it, touch a strange old woman. To our surprise, what we would have called ungentle treatment seemed to silence her, pull her to attention—maybe it was the difference between anxiety and fear.

"OK, Mrs. Best, apple, table, clock," he said.

She gave him a sweet blank look.

"I want you to remember those words, OK? Apple, table, clock. Because before you leave, I'm going to ask you what they were and I want you to be able to tell me, OK?"

"Apple, table, clock," she said.

"Righto. Now how have you been feeling, Mrs. Best?"

"I'm having trouble sleeping," she said.

He looked over at us. "I see your mother's been treated for depression."

"More like mistreated," I said.

He raised an eyebrow. "She has quite a history of medication here. What's she taking for it now?"

"Nothing," said Cathy and went on to explain the episode of hospitalization as a probable overdose and how somewhere along the line, someone had suggested we take her off all psychotropic drugs, to dry her out, as it were, and so we had. And now she was getting more normal by the day, although at some point she might need a little something, the way the elderly often do, quite normally—our father had been taking a little something ever since he started falling asleep in his dinner plate.

I thought it sounded good, the narrative we'd smoothed the last month's lunacy into, the way it even seemed to point to an upbeat ending.

The doctor turned to Mother and in his cranked-up voice, sort of like God from the burning bush, began asking her all the right questions about the President and the month and what state she was from. She looked a little startled each time she answered correctly, but he was nodding his head, and I could sense her feeling better.

Suddenly he shouted, "OK, Mrs. Best, I'd like you to count backwards from 100 by sevens."

Her whole being wilted.

"She's never been good with numbers," I said with a laugh.

He turned my way. "Have you noticed any lapses of memory, any disorientation where—"

"Look, I can't even count forward by sevens," I said. "I don't see how you can expect her to—"

"I meant in general, are we looking at any signs of diminished function that might interfere—"

"Would we be here if our parents' functions weren't diminishing?" Cathy asked calmly. "Isn't that when people normally start looking into continuing care, when they notice a change in their abilities?"

The doctor shrugged. He asked our mother to push against his hands, then pull. Then he gave her a pencil and tablet of paper. "I'd like you to draw a picture for me, Mrs. Best. Do you feel up to that?"

My nerves surged. That would clinch it. "She can draw anything," I said. "Faces, houses in perspective. She's really an artist. Even her doodles you want to frame."

"Don't be silly," Mother said.

But the doctor wasn't even listening. He showed her a simple design, a square within a square, and asked her to copy it. The rest of us sat back, waiting to gloat.

She couldn't manage even one box. What she drew with great effort was a ragged island, a bottomless lake, a balloon that had lost most of its air.

For a minute the doctor didn't say anything. Then he thanked her quietly and took the tablet back.

He had some more tricks, some of which she could perform and some she couldn't. I could tell she was flustered by
her failures, trying to compensate with tremulous docility.
His voice got softer. My own head was screaming alarms: *she
needs* help, *how can we* help *her, who will* help *us now?*

Then it was over, and we were all standing in the hallway
exchanging thank-yous and good-byes and being very polite
and professional, and I felt as if it was happening miles away
because I didn't know what we were going to do, and I was
trying not to cry.

At the door out to the waiting room, Mother halted
and turned and grasped the doctor's arm. With an intake
of breath, her gaze focused, and she was somewhere else, a
receiving line, the Officers' Club, a *command performance.*
"Didn't you forget something?" she asked with polite poise.

"Did I?" he asked back.

"To ask me," she said.

"Ask you?"

"Apple, table, clock," she said.

"OK, righto," he said. "Of course. Apple, table, clock."

4

INDEPENDENT LIVING

It reeked of fresh paint and new carpet, both the grey-white color of paste. The furniture was in place, but unpacked cardboard boxes clogged all four rooms. The box I had just cut open held the contents of our mother's desk. There was no room for her desk in that apartment, or rather we'd decided the "den" should contain our father's desk, and a token pair from his original phalanx of filing cabinets. We were playing with appearance and reality, creating a stage set on which our parents would enact the drama of *Compis Mentis*. For that purpose, one desk would be more than enough.

So where were her papers supposed to go, journals filled with story ideas and beginnings, vignettes and reminiscences, blurted concerns about our father's health and the whereabouts of our brother Bill? Here and there a page turned up a list of things to do: *put up decorations, ask about sciatica, knit, get bran.* Folders contained completed drafts of stories, in which she smoothed over and brightened the struggles of her childhood.

One Friday her father's "ship comes in" at the racetrack, and on Saturday he takes her to Fifth Avenue to buy her a spring coat. They wind up in a carpeted hall of mirrors at Arnold Constable, trying to look as if they belong. The coat she loves costs what he makes in a week at Otis Elevator. He counts out the "weary dollar bills" anyway, and they enjoy flaunting the box on the subway home. In another story, his ship sinks. Then he kneels beside the gas oven, turns it on and sticks his head inside—but just in time her mother comes in from the dumbwaiter to save him.

After a late career teaching English at a small liberal arts college, Mother had spent her retirement typing and retyping these narratives, sending them out to *Good Housekeeping, Woman's Day, Redbook,* where they'd been pronounced a little too depressing in tone. She saved the rejections. One piece had been returned because it touched on death, "a good subject, but one that we have used frequently in the recent past."

She tried a few literary quarterlies at my suggestion, but for those editors her stories were a little too predictable, too smooth. "I wonder how I could have been such a dreamer about my writing," her journal asked. "Dumb! That's me."

Then there was the last piece she probably ever wrote, a report for the monthly meeting of History Club. I remembered her agonizing over it to me on the phone. It had been her turn to provide the program and she didn't feel up to it. She had chosen the State of New York, but it was so big, there was so much written about it, where did you begin? I remembered my impatient patience, slipping into it as automatically as the body braces against cold weather. These women were her friends, I reminded her. They weren't expecting a PBS special. Don't push the panic button, don't fight the problem. Just put your best foot forward.

Now I saw that she had managed to. In a spiral notebook, the handwriting began on the inside of the front cover. What had been once a classic schoolgirl script shivered and stumbled downhill even after it had moved onto the lined pages. Still the sentences rang with the predictable promise she loved: "During the height of the Revolutionary War, General George Washington toured New York and boldly claimed that it would one day become the seat of a new empire. Thus New York received its nickname, the Empire State. At the time it was a backward region, but a brilliant future lay just ahead."

Smeared with erasures, the penciled report moves through demographics into a bit of eighteenth century history before devolving into an alphabetized, annotated list of important people born in the state beginning with Bella Abzug and ending with Catherine Tekakwitha, a Christian Mohawk Indian.

I tried to imagine her reading the information to a circle of women while they nibbled trifle and sipped tea. Did it fool them, her presentation? Did it sound just as reasonable and

relevant to them as last month's report on Nebraska? Or did
her listeners nudge each other? Pick her apart in phone calls
afterward? She'd always been an outsider, a lapsed Catholic
from the East Coast, a latecomer to Main Street, Midwest,
where the other women had lived and faithfully attended
church, Methodist or Lutheran, all their adult lives.

There had probably been a time in Mother's tenuous
membership in their club when she had scoffed behind their
backs at its earnest, random curriculum, a time when she'd
reported meetings to Dad with a smirk and a roll of the eyes.
But it had taken all her psychic and cognitive energy to assemble this data, to push her mind to retrieve what it knew
of organization—topics you invented by some process of ab-
straction which told you which facts to mention in the same
breath. And what effort of the hand to recapture the cursive
rhythms, to honor the convention of the left margin—not to
let it slide insistently to the right—and the convention of horizontal lines—to fight the weight of those loops and curves
that kept dragging them down into your lap.

I wondered whether the normal women noticed her
struggle, whether they applauded her when she was finished
out of habit or charity. Do you dare, after a certain age, judge
the mental competence of your peers?

Probably they never expected a History Club report to be
entertaining. It was just an excuse to polish the silver, bring
out the bone china, and alternate the layers of lady fingers
with fruits and whipped cream. It gave them a reason to open
up the spotless parlors of their Victorian houses, a chance to

lap up praise for the special lace and needlepoint, the refin-
ished armoire.

They all had beautiful things and a special touch with
them. That was a virtue, even to our mother. *Especially* to her.
It was utterly different from the *crass materialism* she decried.
She would have loved to hear it said of her, "She has beautiful things . . . a special touch with them." It would prove an
inborn noblesse, a sort of miracle of nature over nurture in a
child raised in a basement apartment in Yonkers by Emma
and Frank Gonzales, whose second job as the building's su-
per paid the rent.

But now I sat among boxes full of cut glass, crystal,
china, silver, vases and platters, figurines, prints from Japan,
etchings from Germany, oil paintings of flowers, forests, the
sea. Chris and his wife, Lisa, had worked long into the night
to squeeze the furniture into the four rooms. I was in charge
of deploying the beautiful things, but I lacked that elusive
special touch.

It wasn't all going to fit, I could see that. My sister and
brother and I were going to have to take possession of some
of the things ourselves, now rather than later. On visits in
the past; I used to covet them. Or rather I tried to covet
them: to fill up hours of dull moments, I'd survey whatever
room I'd been stuck sitting in, pick out which items I especially liked, maybe picture how they'd look in my rooms
back home. Sometimes I'd just take over their whole adorable
house, throw out all the Ethan Allen furniture, and move my
stuff into it. It made the time pass.

I realized now I didn't want any of it, not at this price. These things were always going to evoke a hollow sadness, a sense that as a family, there had been something we never got to the bottom of, and now the opportunity was lost.

❧

Our parents had seen the apartment empty and they had approved. They had raised eyebrows on cue—*wasn't it nice, the bay window, the balcony, the microwave they were past being able to use?* We were feeling a little more grounded, maybe even smug. We had succeeded in putting something over on Evergreen, which had accepted our patents into its community. The money was down, the contract signed. We belonged. No one would be able to kick us out now.

As we drove them over from Chris's house, we revved ourselves to the point of mania.

"You guys are going to get A's here," I said as Dad poked the giant 3 button in the elevator and we began to rise. We all seemed to get it, we all laughed. "Back home your best efforts were getting you C's if you were lucky, but you'll be valedictorians in a place like this."

Chris slowly pushed open the door from the hallway as if it were the cover of a wonderful book, the heroic story we Bests kept trying to write, the brilliant future lying just ahead. Our parents shuffled in. We waited for the oohs and aahs, the teary smiles. "We have a surprise for you," we'd been telling them. "Wait till you see the surprise we've got for you."

There we stood in the middle of their beautiful things, their furniture arranged almost exactly the way it was in their house in Illinois. If their eyes weren't disappointed, they were blank. Their faces asked, *What surprise? Where's the surprise?*

"We thought maybe it would be Billy," Mother said.

At first I was hurt, then angry. It was too familiar, that insertion of our missing brother, like a zero denominator, blowing everything apart. Billy sober and employed, Billy at his debonair best returned to serenade us in his haunting Whiffenpoof tenor: was that the only scenario worthy of the term *surprise?* When was she going to acknowledge reality?

But when were we? The same chairs they'd had trouble getting out of, the same console TV with its impenetrable VCR, the shelves of books they couldn't follow for more than a paragraph—what kind of surprise was that? What was our father supposed to do at his big oak desk, sit and mourn his inability to add and subtract? Push a mechanical pencil across the pad on his clipboard for show? Pretend that his upright, absolutely regular handwriting, with its generous loops on the final Y's and G's, had bunched up into knots we could hardly read?

Evenings came the test. Could they match sweaters with skirts, ties with jackets? Could they remember zippers and get the buttons in the corresponding holes? Could they engage in reasonable conversation, could they choose appropriate items in an appropriate order from the salad bar—*no sliced peaches on top of tomatoes, put the croutons on last, just a few.* Could they carry their plates across the dining room without mishap and eat without spilling food on their clothes? Were they as worried about these things as they had taught me to be?

Dad printed the day's date on the palm of his hand in washable ink. He carried their apartment and phone numbers on a card in his pants pocket. Now that Mother's medications were under control, her repartee held few surprises. When another resident asked her how she was, she could respond smoothly and predictably without a pause. If now and then she chatted about imagined visits from old friends, encounters with children, sightings of cats, no one but Dad was any wiser.

When I drove down from DC once a month, I played the game with them. In the dining room decked out like a fine restaurant, I smiled radiantly into the stares of other residents. I slowed down to Dad and Mother's pace, offered help calmly, pushed stray chairs in out of the way front of them, stowed Dad's cane, picked up his fallen napkin, praised the wonderful food. The larger tables always sat four of five elegantly dressed couples bubbling with cocktails and conviviality, cliques of the least diminished, most normal, which our parents would never have been asked to join—which was fine. Under such pressure they would probably have buckled.

It all came to seem a matter of luck, whether you were pushed into the dining room in a wheelchair by your spouse or hobbled in shoving a walker or pranced in wearing a silk suit and high heels; whether you were bloated with medication, hooked to oxygen, or sun-tanned and just back from a holiday on Aruba.

As it was also just by luck that one tiny widow's son was a presidential advisor who had been on the cover of *Time* magazine. Spry in her pink dress and pumps, she entered the dining room to the buzz of whispering—*there she goes, so-and-so's mother, doesn't she look just like him, they say she's very nice, not at all a snob.*

Space would have been made for her in a flash at any of the large tables. When the famous son himself showed up and joined her at a table for two, the whole room sucked in its breath and went quiet.

It was enough to make every other parent feel envious; deficient, every other visiting child.

༚

Month after month, Dad greeted me with the same news: "You know, it's slipped my mind how to work the VCR." He seemed to accept the fact that his days of taping from TV were over, but he had his beloved stash of old movies—if only he could remember how to get the tapes to play. Clipboard in hand, he asked, "How about you check me out?"

I knew that Chris, who visited daily, went over the procedure almost as often. But I was a teacher and refused to admit there wasn't a mind I couldn't unlock.

I made a list of the steps, and when that didn't help, I broke down the steps into ever more limited ones: sit in the middle of the sofa; point the grey end of the remote toward the TV; place one finger on the word POWER; push. When these instructions still didn't help, I numbered all the buttons

involved with squares of adhesive. When Cathy got the same
news on her visits, she tried magic markers of different colors.

The television continued to shimmer with mystery.
When the Evergreen bus took them to Krogers, they bought
a TV GUIDE out of habit, but there was no correspondence
between its programming and the channels on their cable.
Mother complained that they could only pick up one channel, and that was in Spanish.

When I was there, we went through their tapes of Er-
rol Flynn, James Stewart, Claudette Colbert. I tried renting
movies for variety, choosing carefully for PG-13 stories with
happy endings. Dad fell asleep watching. Mother seemed at-
tentive, but afterwards decided enigmatically, "I didn't like
all that sex."

One month I remembered to check the TV listings in the
DC area, and had caught a juicy film on tape—Fred Astaire
and Ginger Rogers. At dinner when I told them about the
special treat I'd brought, Mother said, "He always had a
crush on Ginger Rogers. He would have married her instead
of me if she'd have had him."

Dad protested. He'd never wanted anyone but Mommy.

"What about Gloria?" she asked.

"You had that Spanish kid. What was his name?"

Her eyes twinkled. "Which one?"

They were getting in the mood. Upstairs, they settled
side by side on the sofa holding hands. They hadn't a care in
the world. I was there, and had the monster of technology
under control.

I slipped in the tape and punched *play*. Instead of romance, music, dancing that defied gravity, mortality, we got talking heads—oily jowls and big noses, harshly made-up eyes. It took me a few minutes to realize I'd recorded a meeting of the Montgomery County Council.

We looked at each other in silence. They were disappointed, but their faces showed more vindication than surprise. Now did I see? What had they been trying to tell me?

"I guess you're not the only ones," I said.

༄

I was not going to let our mother turn into her mother.

Grandma Gonzales used to sit in her mahogany rocker at the apartment window and never go out. When we kids piled out of the station wagon for a Yonkers visit, we'd look up to that window and there would be the pale moon of her face. Grandpa took us down the hill to play in Trevor Park and view the stuffed elephant that was the centerpiece of its small museum, or we all plodded up the hill to the drugstore on Warburton Avenue for a coke.

We left Grandma sitting in the rocker. Though we returned to the smell of sautéed garlic and a gigantic meal waiting to be served, there she'd be, just as we'd left her, in the chair, a mound of grandmother, a litany of ailments, a pair of martyred eyes.

My mother, I'd decided, was going to go for walks. She was going to try the equipment in the exercise room and swim in the indoor pool. At least when I was visiting.

She didn't want to do any of these things.

"I have one of my head-aches," she'd say. "I feel a little dizzy. I'm so tired. It's too windy. Maybe tomorrow."

I overrode the anxiety. She was enjoying extra desserts in the dining room. The skeletal, post-psychotic woman whom we'd smuggled into the apartment a few months ago had plumped up, grown soft to the touch. Her Pendleton skirts were looking snug. She had to get some exercise. It was her anxiety or mine.

She had always been agile, a strong, fast walker. Physically, she'd never acted old. Dad used to joke about the Saturday mornings she'd ask him to help her in the garden. They'd sit down and compile the list he couldn't make a move without, but by the time he'd figured the order in which to approach each task, assembled wheelbarrow, shovel, work gloves, whatever, made the pitcher of iced tea, she had all the jobs practically done.

So I bundled her up and dragged her around the maze of corridors, talking louder when she asked, "Can't we go back now?" We tried an *expeditio* to Dillard's with a mission to focus on, buying Dad undershirts, and when that was accomplished, I kept calling her attention to some other exhibit of merchandise, just a few steps further, just a few minutes more in the outside world, as though the banal, glitzy profusion of a shopping mall were tonic, a cause for less panic rather than more.

One afternoon we were wandering the lower levels of Evergreen looking for the exercise room, and she was hanging back, her eyes growing rounder, as if it were a scene from a thriller and an assassin lurked behind the next turn.

"It's OK, Mom," I kept saying—more of that impatient patience. "We're not lost. If it isn't this hallway, it'll be the next one. Isn't this nice carpet? I like the pattern. Take some deep belly breaths, Mom. We're almost there."

There turned out to be a bunch of rubber mats, a stair-climber that didn't work and two stationary bikes side by side. They had also seen better days. But then, so had we.

I adjusted one seat to fit Mother; she held her breath as if I were defusing a bomb. Then I helped her climb on. Shakily she pushed on the pedals and they rotated to the sound of metal grating against metal. I did the same, looking down my shoulder at her with a big smile. Her lips were pressed together, her eyes were on her feet.

"I can feel my heart beating," she said after pedaling for a minute or two.

"That's good," I said. "That means you're getting aerobic benefits."

Her eyes lifted to mine. "I don't like my heart to beat this fast," she gasped and finally her terror leaped the gap between us. I couldn't deflect it. I helped her climb down.

I put my arm around her hunched shoulders. We shuffled back to the elevator like defeated troops. For a moment I recognized my own cruelty, the masquerade of my need as hers. "I'm sorry," I said. "I don't know what I was thinking."

But the awareness didn't last.

꧁꧂

She had everything she needed—a dressmaker swimsuit draped in the right places, a bathing cap covered in rubber petals, swim shoes made of rubber and mesh. She and Dad both had terrycloth robes to wrap up in for the journey downstairs to the pool and back. And when we pushed open the door into its chlorinated humidity, we saw that we had it all to ourselves.

I was not going to pressure her. An outing was an outing, whether she spent it examining the tropical plants by the window or venturing a paddle in the pool. Meanwhile, I'd brought my goggles—figuring I could get in some laps.

I hopped into the tepid water and sidestroked past her on the deck.

"How is it?" she called.

"Refreshing." I put my face in and switched to the crawl.

She took ages to remove her robe and pull the cap of pink petals down over her ears. "I don't know about my sinuses," she told me from the ladder. "Sometimes I wake up in the night and I can hardly breathe."

I pushed off for the deep end again.

Through my goggles, I saw Dad face down in the water, face down but not horizontal. His arms and legs dangled underneath him like a jellyfish. I stopped to make sure he was all right. His white hair floated on the surface around the back of his head like a long fringe. The motion of his arms and legs advanced his body a few feet, then he put his feet on the bottom, eyes squeezed shut against his dripping hair, gulped a breath, then fell forward face down again.

His determination was almost suicidal—he would fight the pain in his legs, the paralysis of Parkinson's disease with everything he had. He really was shooting for an A in aging, doing everything he should. He walked twice a day, gripping his cane so hard he had trouble letting go when it was time to put it down. He was the only male to attend a weekly Yoga class, which was making Mother jealous.

"So why don't you take yoga too?" I'd asked.

"He's the one who could dance, not me."

"Yoga isn't the foxtrot. It's exercise."

"Why would I want to watch those widows fawning all over him?" she said. "You should see them yoo-hoo him in the dining room. They're so obvious."

I think she also envied the yoga instructor. She was a resident of Evergreen, but not at all the typical resident, a bit of a go-getter, when you thought about it—she had volunteered to put together the yoga class and teach it. Small and lithe with straight white hair bobbed short with bangs, she wore a funny hat with the brim rolled back, block-printed tunics over black pants, and no make-up. She looked artistic, a little bohemian. If not *spiritual*, at least a free spirit.

Our mother might have wanted to be just like her, and could have been, with a little more courage, a little less concern for what other people thought. Or maybe the flickering wish was mine. *If our mother were more like the yoga teacher, would we be where we are now?*

Dad was on all fours on the paste-colored carpet in their living room, then he was sitting, then he had rolled onto his stomach and was lifting his chin, moving his arms, then he was on all fours again, pushing back onto his haunches and rising from a knee bend. When he was upright again, he gave slight hop, to punctuate his performance, a hop he would never have been able to accomplish if he'd set himself to try just it alone—it was a last flaring of the energy the yoga movement has released.

He looked surprised and proud to be back on his feet. I felt proud of him too, his refusal to give up. Hadn't he gotten Mother onto the Evergreen bus for a trip to Duke Chapel on Martin Luther King Day? Didn't I still find the barely legible beginnings of lists around the apartment: *nail clippers, Clorets, call Chris, pictures, Tommy toilet*?

Tommy was the head of maintenance whom our father decided he'd better consult after Mother ate her wedding ring. At least that's what she'd told us she'd done, all puzzled innocence herself: it just slid off her finger one day, and she felt the overwhelming conviction that she should swallow it. It was days afterward that she mentioned it, too late to watch her stool for the glint of gold. But there was the long shot, the hope, that maybe it was still somewhere in the plumbing. Dad had gotten Tommy upstairs to check.

No, he hadn't given up. His own mild delusions provoked by Mother's had subsided. He tried to make and grasp sense, even though more and more of his statements trailed off into silence.

"He'll have to come back to that," Mother would say when that happened, coaching him. Twice she'd felt up to attending a support group for spouses of Parkinson's sufferers, and that was what she'd managed to remember, not to let him brood over sentences without ends.

"I've got a head full of cotton," Dad said. "When I try to think, it goes all blurry and white."

On my visit in late spring, he told me of his hikes to the little man-made pond. "I walk right along the edge," he said. "I come pretty close."

I pictured his unsteady balance, his clumsy, too-big shoes, then that little hop, all it would take. Again I turned away from the vision as too theoretical, a stab at bravado, a flimsy shield against all the evidence that there was nothing to be done. Life wasn't a learning experience. It was merely experience.

"We've hit bottom," he said. "I don't know how we're going to get . . . Do you think this is any kind of life?"

"No," I said. "I think life should be something else—not this difficult, not this unfair. My heart aches for you both."

He was silent, groping around in the white blur.

I was afraid I'd said too much. "But you do seem to be making something good of it," I went on. "I give you a lot of credit for having the guts to try."

"I've got to stick around for Mommy," he said. "She can't manage without me."

"I need you alive too. I love seeing you, now that you're only a few hours away."

My words floated above us like balloons untethered to anything real. Before and after my visits, I dragged for days. And why should he have to endure life just for us? Why should he have to keep mustering energy for efforts that led nowhere, that at best slightly slowed his course down the slippery slope? I was asking the question he'd raised me to ask, *Where was the point?*

We were up against something a Best could not fathom, existence without a future, without promise of advancement, the boundaries of a script we hadn't written and were helpless to change or control.

Chris, the scientist, still dared to hope for improvement, if not full restoration, through the strict oversight of our parents' meds. Sloppy malpractice in that department had tipped us into what he called The Vortex. Maybe with careful control and documentation of what our parents swallowed, we could correlate inputs and outcomes, wiggle variables, and claw our way out.

But their regimen of pills was still too complicated for them to execute by themselves. So we bought plastic dispensers with compartments marked with the days of the week and times of day. Chris spent an hour every Sunday filling them, and he checked them when he visited during the week.

Pretty soon, he'd begun finding the wrong lids open, their compartments empty. Lectures and demonstrations didn't seem to help. Our parents complained that the lids

fit too tightly. On Tuesday morning, the little door marked
Tuesday morning just wouldn't open, and they had to pry at
a lot of other doors until they hit one that did.

Chris shifted to a matrix of labeled test tubes propped
in a frame. You simply tipped the correctly marked test-tube
into your hand, and *voila*, your pills. After the first month,
the test tubes also began to turn up empty in no particular
order. There was no way to tell who was taking what.

Chris contacted the executive director of Evergreen to
ask if we could pay someone to administer our parents' meds.
She said we could, for almost $3000 more per month. A reli-
able young man who worked in Chris's lab offered to do the
job on the weekdays for considerably less.

The executive director fussed for a while about compro-
mised security with a stranger walking in and out of the
building all the time, but the system seemed to work. And
Chris drove in to Evergreen three times a day on the week-
ends, except for the once a month when Cathy and I visited,
when we could take charge.

Cathy and I had finally conceded that it was too much
for either one of us alone to maneuver two disabled bodies in and out of the car, in and out of the doors and chairs
of a restaurant. Forty-eight hours straight of our parents'
worries, ailments, frustrations, and sleepless wandering had
turned monthly stays in their extra bedroom into nightmare
ordeals. Although our parents got fewer visits now that we
came down together to see them, we weren't dreading the
trips as much. We were finding more occasions to laugh, all

four of us, and the return drive gave Cathy and me hours to talk, to go over every detail until its current of shock and sorrow was discharged.

Now it was summer and we were preparing for an *expeditio* to Duke Gardens to see if any day lilies were still blooming. I was clearing away the bags and papers from our lunch sandwiches. Cathy was remembering the meds. We didn't always. We could remind each other and remind each other up to half an hour before it was time for a dose, and then, much to Chris's chagrin, we could still forget.

But this time Cathy had filled a glass with water and was holding the pills out to Mother, who was stubbornly shaking her head. We assumed she was objecting to the excursion. She had already declared that she didn't want to go out, not even if the destination were flowers, she had been to the Duke Gardens plenty of times, it was too hot, she didn't want to put on sun-block, and she didn't like all the hills.

And we hadn't listened. We couldn't. She was the one who'd taught us to love gardening. We didn't want to imagine the internal ruin that had robbed the garden of its appeal, turned the sacred marriage of art and nature into something she could take or leave.

"Come on," Cathy coaxed, "we've got to get you ready. Look, just three little ones, one big swallow . . ."

I was searching the rack of test-tubes for Dad's pills. "Wait," I said, just as Mother popped the three little ones into her mouth and took a gulp from the glass. "Aren't these hers?" I held up a different tube.

"I don't know, are they?" Cathy swooped over, peered at the labels, looked up and met my eyes. I couldn't help clutching my throat. I felt like throwing up. "Oh god," Cathy said.

I dragged her into the guest bedroom and closed the door. "What'll we do? What if we've poisoned her?"

"Three pills aren't going to poison her. But maybe we should call the Wellness Clinic."

"What can we say?" I was mortified. I'd been entrusted with something fragile then gone and broken it. "And what are going to tell Chris?"

"We'll just have to tell him the truth."

"But without her hearing."

Cathy went back to the living room and with the intense matter-of-factness of someone evacuating a building because of a bomb threat, got out their jackets and began helping them put them on. She cocked her head at me, and I slipped into the den, gave the door a casual slam behind me, picked up the phone and tried to force myself into the over-stuffed closet. When Chris answered, I whispered the news, that something horrible had happened.

I wanted him to say, *Don't worry, nothing can be that horrible*, but I knew we didn't believe that anymore, and instead I heard, "Uh oh."

I blurted our mistake.

He gave a groan.

"I am so sorry. After all you've been doing to take care of them, all your efforts, and we just blow it in one second of careless—"

"The Vortex," he muttered.

"What should we do? Is there anything?"

"Forget about it. She'll survive. You think she hasn't taken his pills plenty of times before?"

ﷻ

Spruce Assisted Living needed bodies. Sometime before Thanksgiving, Chris saw the item in the Evergreen newsletter: the facility that occupied the lower wing of the building was only half-full and thus operating at a loss. This impacted on other important items in the Evergreen budget, like landscaping and decorating and arts and crafts supplies. If residents of the apartments or cottages had friends on the outside who needed extra help maintaining the quality of their lives, they should encourage them to apply directly to Spruce, and their applications would be given serious consideration.

Within days of reading this Chris received a call from the executive director informing him that our parents were no longer capable of managing in *independent* living and would have to be moved to *assisted* living downstairs.

They had flunked out.

It was a moment of such truth it forced blindness. It announced the sort of battle a Best can't resist: righteous, life-or-death, losing.

We were outraged. We had come to identify our devotion to our parents with our ability to keep them out of anything resembling a nursing home. We were defending general principles, a simple Braille: they had been violently uprooted once, and now they should be allowed to stay in their apartment no matter how much behind-the-scenes intervention and coaching this dignity required.

Weren't they getting down to the dining room once a day without a hitch? Weren't they taking the bus to Krogers and buying their weekly bananas, instant oatmeal, prune juice, and big packages of those generic vanilla cookies with vanilla filling which our father loved? Didn't they produce money at the checkout to pay? Didn't they more or less remember doctor's appointments?

Thanks, but no thanks, Chris told the executive director. We had a system in place, which more or less worked.

The executive director kept up the pressure. We'd blown our cover, Chris decided, when he'd asked her about help with medications some months back. After a meeting with her, he was even more furious. Her only qualification for running Evergreen was her status as the wife of one of the doctors on the founding board. Now here she was trying to tell him that she was not only more qualified than he was to make decisions about our parents' welfare but also more genuinely, more unselfishly concerned about them than we were.

Chris stopped returning her calls. By phone Cathy and I shored his resolve. We reminded ourselves that no one could be sure our mother really had Alzheimer's. She had always been a little zany. Our father had gotten slower, feebler, over the course of the year, and he'd never been one to suffer gracefully, but he was hanging in there. What did the executive director know? Her heart was in decorating, her mind was on money. She was Marie Antoinette and Evergreen was her play farm. She had no concept of the needs and fears enfolded in those bodies upon whose failure her profits depended.

The more we dwelt on the director's weaknesses, the stronger our parents seemed. We still imagined that their final passage could be gentle, imperceptible, not some jerky rite of expulsion decreed by a corporate bottom line.

Then one evening after work when he swung by the apartment for his daily visit, Chris found our parents sitting on the couch, Mother with a smile of relief on her face, Dad close to tears. Would they like him to help them get ready for dinner, Chris asked.

"I don't think we'll be going to dinner anymore," Dad said, his thin voice breaking.

"I'm awfully glad you finally showed up," said Mother.

"Mommy needs a doctor," Dad said.

Chris took a deep, patient breath. "What seems to be the problem?"

"I realize this whole thing means a lot to you, sweetie," Mother began.

"What whole thing is that?" Chris asked.

"My staying in this lovely apartment with him."

"You mean Dad?"

"I realize he's a perfectly nice man, but he just doesn't belong here."

"See what I mean?" moaned Dad.

"Look, you guys." Chris had to grab the back of a chair, he told us an hour later on the phone, because the floor was beginning to rotate under his feet.

"She says she never met me," Dad cried.

"He expects me to make conversation," Mother said, smiling—sweetly, mysteriously, triumphantly? Chris couldn't describe her smile.

"I give up," Dad said.

Chris was ready to give up too.

~ 5 ~

ASSISTED LIVING

As if a battle were over, the smoke started to clear. We had surrendered our parents' five rooms on the third floor in exchange for two adjacent rooms in Spruce Assisted Living Center, one level below the main.

No more den with abandoned desk and filing cabinets.

No more kitchen equipped with appliances that neither parent could remember how to use.

No more extra bedroom; no more charade of guests and hosts.

No more master bedroom with king-sized bed. Our parents would be sleeping henceforth in separate metal beds that cranked up and down and came with guard rails.

Evergreen's concessions: we could wait until after the holidays to make the transition, and they would cut a door between the two rooms at our expense, as long as we took care of walling it up when our parents . . . when our parents no longer resided there.

The first Saturday morning in the new year, bright and brittle cold, found Cathy and me hurtling down Interstate 85, an endless slice through endless pines beyond reach of NPR. We listened over and over to a tape Cathy had ordered for inspiration, a new perspective. Its title was *Death is Not an Outrage*, and its wise voice assured us that since the body came and went, nothing mattered except an open heart.

It didn't really help. Even if the material world was all an illusion, insignificant, we still couldn't help worrying about our parents' tiny sector of it, the pain of paring away more layers of clothes, papers, books, familiar, beautiful objects from their fragile lives.

We arrived at Evergreen to find that someone forgot to order the creation of the all-important door between their new rooms. Their move would have to be postponed until the next weekend, when Cathy I would have to make the five-hour drive again.

The following Saturday came, and we had hurtled, listened, and worried some more. Now as we gathered and boxed possessions in our parents' apartment, we talked up the new arrangement. We called it a *suite*—one room for the sofa, a chair, a bookcase, and TV, the other for their beds and dressers. Who really needed anything more? Mother, pinned in the present moment, tried to oblige with enthusiasm. Dad, still capable of history, looked woeful but maintained a stalwart silence.

Cathy and I left them sitting side by side on their couch in order to wheel a loaded dolly along the labyrinthine corridors to the far end of the building and the gateway to abandoned hope, the elevator which the upstairs residents tried to smile and forget—an elevator that only went down.

The décor below mimicked the programmed elegance of the décor above, more mauve and forest green, a small dining room containing eight tables draped in white linen and sporting a central carnation, a communal parlor with the potpourri smell of a gift shop and sofas upholstered in vinyl chintz. On the coffee table a book delivered its title like a punch line—*Think Big: Unleashing your Potential for Excellence*, written by some MD.

In our parents' *suite* we found a carpenter hammering raw woodwork into place around a just-cut passage. Sawdust and drywall littered the carpet. What was going on, we wanted to know? "We were told a month ago—not *told*, more like *ordered*—to move our parents to this space last week only to find nothing ready for them," Cathy began. "Now here we are and here's this, this mess, what are you guys thinking? Is anyone thinking?"

My own vocal cords were straining not to scream the words it seems no one ever has a right to: *this isn't fair.*

The carpenter shrugged. No one had told him he was cutting a door until a couple hours ago, called him at home, promised him time and a half.

"Just go ahead and work around him," the executive director said when Cathy got her on the phone.

"But what about the dirty carpet? And the doorway's got to be painted, and the walls touched up."

"We'll get to it. We've got work orders in."

"Our parents can't live here on wet carpet with wet paint," Cathy said. "What about the fumes? These are the people you said need *special* care. Is this what you call special care?"

"Suit yourself, if you want to wait another week."

"If we suited ourselves, they'd stay in their apartment."

The executive director said, "The rooms will be as good as new by the day after tomorrow."

So we marched back to the other mess upstairs to wait.

Mother didn't want to hear the anger she could sense we were bottling. She tried to make us feel better. Maybe the change was easiest on her, her bearings by now so lost, what was one more pitch or heave on a rough crossing? She could still talk, still try to explain: "They put Daddy on the dog list because he doesn't dress right."

The strange man had become Daddy when we'd started to pack. "Unless you believe in God and wear the right clothes," she went on, "they admonish you in a letter. Now if he can just get his voice back and his sense back, we'll have a nice long talk."

Yes, Mother. Dear Mother, retired officer's wife, little woman behind the man—such creative passivity. Once more it would help her survive.

She saw our lips twitch toward smiles and thinking she had cheered us, said, "I'm starting to have the feelings of a person who has a problem but who's going to lick it."

Our father, whose speech was bound more tightly to facts and actions, remained silent. He still clung to real life, even though a minute's worth of it was taking him five. I knew it was a struggle for him to keep up with conversations around him. Months before, as the presidential election wound down, he'd offered the simple observation at dinner, "This Ross Perot guy holds some interesting viewpoints."

I'd taken it as a familiar call to arms, shrieking, "How can you say that?" and rattling off half a dozen reasons why I thought Perot was an irresponsible maniac. Hadn't the dinner table always been a site of harangue and debate?

Not anymore. Dad's face went blank, confused, a look between panic and plea. What was I trying to do to him? When was I going to understand?

I ached to tell him I was sorry, for not recognizing the effort behind his stab at political analysis, for demanding more. But I'd been afraid to make the moment worse.

On top of his growing debility, he never knew what his wife was going to say next, nor was he sure, when her words made no sense, whether the problem was in her brain or his. It didn't help, I realize now, that my sister and I had grown lax in correcting her imaginings.

"I'm mentioned in the newsletter as the new English teacher," she would tell us.

"That's nice," we'd say.

"But I haven't even been given the assignment!"

"Just be patient. These things take time."

Better for Dad when Chris was around, sacred son, fel-

low scientist. He scorned the path of least resistance and up-
held the facts. "Now Mom," he said. "You used to be a very
fine English teacher, and then you retired, and now you don't
have to worry about the responsibilities of a job."

৩৸৩

Having decided to recognize our father as her husband,
she began to suspect his fidelity. On that subject all three of
us children stood firm.

"He has his heart on another woman," she confided to
me. "And he's going to get stung."

"That's absurd," I told her. "You are the love of Dad's life.
Always have been and always will be."

"He almost died when I said I was going to tell you."

"I'll bet he did. Because it isn't true, and it hurts him
deeply to hear you say things like that."

"I said I'd do it in a palatable way." She sounded subdued,
contrite. "Of course it's starvation for men when they can't
have a sex life. They all want one, if they have the normal ac-
coutrements. They have no sense of shame."

Where did it come from, the fantasized triangle, and the
disdain for the male appetite? When did we ever mention *sex
lives* in our house? Sex, maybe, rarely, in the stable terms of
anatomy and physiology.

But *sex life*—such innuendo, quivering with pleasure,
politics, romance?

Loss of inhibitory reflex, Cathy suggested. She'd heard of
it happening. I preferred *the return of the repressed*. Or maybe

just *swansong*, before the sexual forces that spin this illusion of a world release one more body into the peace of the soul.

Anyway, labeling helped. It boosted us onto the high ground of theory. We could ditch unwelcome images. But it didn't help our father, who must have felt that he was losing her all over again, along with everything else.

On Monday evening, we made a dinner *expeditio* to Mc-Donald's for quarter-pounders with cheese and milkshakes, one of his favorite meals. Then we led them downstairs.

The new rooms smelled of chemicals. Dad glanced at the familiar furnishings. "Look, everyone," I called out, "there was just enough space for the china cabinet. See—all Mom's beautiful things." But he'd moved on to the other room—the two metal beds, a five-foot chasm in between. With great formality, he pronounced the suite very nice and thanked us for all our help. Then he turned toward the window and let out a sob.

He'd seen what he could no longer retrieve the words to express—words hard and tight as seeds among the cotton he said filled his brain: life was about to become intolerable.

People would begin speaking to him in artificial voices, their suggestions disguising orders, their questions become rhetorical. His answers wouldn't matter anymore. Almost all these people would be women, women trying to be patient, but it would be an effort they couldn't hide. He would begin to feel like an object, breakable, maybe explosive. He'd begin to feel like a chore, a child of a harried mother, an allotment of minutes during someone's shift.

He'd have to sign out to go outdoors. His daily walks would be timed, watched. He'd be suspected of wanting to wander off, to stumble out the door and keep on going until he dropped.

He would eat in the little dining room that provided bibs, then shuffle back to his own shrunken territory, where his quiet would be interrupted according to a schedule he wouldn't be able to grasp, by women announcing music appreciation, church services, women suggesting that he brush his teeth, comb his hair, daring to ask if he needed to use the bathroom, women bearing paper cups of pills, plastic pitchers of the same drinking water he is perfectly capable of drawing himself from the tap.

And the wife he'd devoted his life to, on whose behalf he had striven and accomplished, whom he'd come to rely on for daily sympathy and support, his wife had fallen into an appalling hole of dirty language and thoughts. She was calling him a *tailhound*—when had she ever heard such an expression? For no reason she would start telling the kids horrible things, that he had no sense of shame, when that was one of the few things he would never lose.

Sometimes when he dozed almost comfortably in the easy chair, she would lean over him and whisper in his ear, "I'll understand, Bill, if you're in love with someone else. I can forgive you. Go be with her. It's enough that one of us will find happiness."

That first day our father felt a change in the air, and supposed a front moving in, a gathering storm, the winds of war.

Spruce Unit was practically empty, as we'd guessed from the executive director's sudden determination to get our parents moved down, but within a month they were joined by the similarly demoted Marie, a woman with hair so white and radiant she looked holy, an elderly angel blessed with a wardrobe of muted blues and purples which she could still assemble stunningly.

Our mother was not happy to see her. Marie's apartment upstairs had been a couple doors down from our parents'. She used to catch them in the hallway and talk and talk, and they had a hard time breaking away.

"She whispers," Mom complained. "I can hardly understand a word she says. She's a woman widowed early in the season who takes her widowhood seriously. I think she has a drink every other day."

To these past offenses, Mom now added the suspicion that Marie was more interested in our father than in her. When Marie comes over to our table in the dining room, sure enough, there is a sleepy droop to her eyelids that might at one time have whispered sensuality, and she did grip our father's arm—but less, it seemed, to invite romance than to hold him in place for an exchange of courtesies.

Her lips nibbled the air for a few seconds before she actually spoke. "It must be nice to have sisters and brothers to fall apart and come back together," she said nodding at Cathy and me.

Mother would have liked to give her the cold shoulder, but a stronger impulse won, to prove that she still deserved the title, *conversationalist*, which Dad had always bestowed on her with slightly patronizing respect. "Thank goodness there's a place here," she said, "where they give you free food if you pay."

Cathy and I understood exactly what she meant: rather than be charged twelve dollars apiece for dinners ordered from the kitchen, we had taken to running upstairs to the cafeteria, shelling out a couple dollars for the very same meal, and carrying it down on trays to the Spruce dining room.

Marie seemed to understand too. She and Mom continued to circle the subjects of family and food until Marie gave Dad a series of hard pats and said, "Well, I'd better go and get indoctrinated. After eight they make you stay all night."

Next month's visit we found two more rooms occupied by new residents, Louise and Tom, the one friendly, fluent, the other more shy, but responsive to social overtures. Both were nicely dressed and groomed, confident with knife and fork. Tom had spring in his step, and Louise tromped around on the well-defined calves of a thirty-year-old in wooden Dr. Scholl's sandals. If not Olympic athletes, they seemed to be scoring pretty high on the age curve, yet there had to be things wrong with them, or else why were they there?

We tried to pump our parents, but the newcomers were unknown quantities, having been admitted straight from the outside world. Even Mom had the sense not to pretend to have the goods on them.

The next month a man and a woman in their forties accompanied Tom into the dining room. They tried not to

stare at Cathy and me, and we tried not to stare at them
as we all four tried to figure out what was wrong, and with
whom. It occurred to me that I could have been mistaken
for a resident—I had a full head of grey hair, while brunette
Louise at the next table hadn't a single strand. I addressed our
parents loudly as Mom and Dad. It seemed very important to
keep us all sorted out.

But a month later, Tom's room was empty. Mom told
us he'd died, then on second thought remembered that this
quiet, sheepish man had been kicked out because he'd gone
berserk and torn his room apart. We asked a nurse, who said
tersely that his family had moved him somewhere else.

When Cathy and I ran up to the cafeteria for our trays
of food, we came panting back to the little dining room to
find our parents well into their meals and an elfin man with
flaring ears perched at their table for four. They stopped grappling with their forks for a moment, long enough to throw us
martyred looks: how could we have expected them to tell this
stranger that the seat he took was already taken?

As they resumed eating, he introduced himself, reached
for his cane and offered to move. Cathy and I wouldn't hear
of it. We dragged up a fifth chair and squeezed in along the
table's vacant side.

Roger's wife lived in Virginia, but he was in Durham to
be near his daughter because he'd had a hip replacement. He
was interested in all the places we had lived, knew everything
about geography and climate, and proudly returned several
times to the fact that a major problem in his life, inconti-

nence, had now been solved by having his bathroom only a few steps from his bed. It all sort of made sense, and Roger's adept transitions were a relief from our mother's leaps and our father's silence. In fact, our parents' envy of his coherence was palpable, masquerading as envy often does as contempt.

But afterwards we wondered. Was that wife of his really alive? Did his daughter exist? If he were upstairs, we wouldn't even question it. But down a level he couldn't be trusted. As our mother had observed, in one of her flashes of insight that always caught us off guard, "You say one thing crazy and they never believe you after that."

Meanwhile, Louise lost her temper when she was delivered a dinner with no dessert. One of the staff explained that she could have her dessert after she ate some of her vegetables and meat. "That slop?" she snarled. "It's absolutely unfit for consumption. I wouldn't feed it to pigs."

The staff member explained that she needed to eat something besides sugar to stay strong and healthy. Louise wanted to know why, since she had nothing to stay strong and healthy for—she'd gotten rid of her husband long ago and her family had deserted her. "They're doing everything they can to get their hands on my money," she said loudly. "I wish I could die and save them the trouble." Then she stomped out of the dining room and up and down the two intersecting corridors of the unit. A half hour later we could still hear the slap-clunk, slap-clunk of her Dr. Scholl's.

That night, unable to sleep, Cathy and I recalled the polished surfaces of the upstairs residents, how critical we used to be of their have-a-nice-day smiles, their vacant courtesies. Why weren't they holding consciousness-raising groups, we'd wondered, sharing their needs and fears about the end of life instead of hiding them? Now we were beginning to understand how much surface became substance when you stood on the brink of the slippery slope. The conventions of the social theatre got strictly enforced, and who you were was how well you played your part. Personality, pathos, profundity—those things didn't count unless you delivered your scripted lines without a hitch.

It was all performance. Humankind wasn't a family, it was both a troupe, an ensemble, and an audience. In some fractured way, maybe Mother had been trying to tell us this when she kept reporting her exploits on stage and screen. Since starring in that dramatic version of *Connecticut Yankee*, she'd stolen the show in an ad for toilet paper, for which she'd provided the voice-over for the little girl who stood in front of the camera and moved her mouth. We also heard about the play she attended, where "they got up on the stage, turned their backs to the audience and proceeded to read softly," and the play she was writing herself, her work-in-progress, ominously entitled *The End of Willie*.

"Willie Best here," Dad used to answer the phone. He was being folksy, one of the guys. Back when he was healthy, that was a role he enjoyed.

Now he played another, as if he'd made up his mind: *if*

*we're supposed to need special care, then by George, we're going
to be sure we get it.*

He stopped trying to make his way outside twice a day
for a walk. The swimming pool and the room for yoga, the
ageless yoga teacher, like bright signs of life on a receding
planet, faded from his mind's eye. His teeth began to hurt,
which meant several trips to the dentist with Chris to complete a root canal. He barked a shin on the metal bed frame,
and instead of healing, it remained an oozing wound. He
couldn't see with his old glasses anymore, which meant a trip
to the optometrist with Chris but no change of prescription.
We figured out that his bifocals were sliding down his nose,
and he was trying to read through the distance lens. We ex-
perimented with bands to hold the glasses in place, and we
tried to show him that tilting his head up made a big difference, but we realized that something as simple as a slight
lift of the head was almost beyond a body succumbing to
Parkinson's, and reading might anyway be beyond his brain.

The pain in his side from intestinal scar tissue sparked
daily attacks of anxiety, a reflowering of the cancer suspicions
he'd harbored for twenty years. To Chris he blurted a desperate secret: as a small child he had been plunked down on
the toilet every morning and forbidden to do anything else
until he performed. He remembered how helpless and hopeless he'd felt sitting there alone, tuned to the distant sounds
of the world going on without him.

Chris worked daily to relax and reassure him, to rout his
certainty that his body hid something malignant. But every

morning it returned full force. Finally Chris scheduled him for a sigmoidoscopy over at Duke, on a Saturday when Cathy and I would be there to take him. Of course our mother would go along.

In her effort to match Dad ailment for ailment, symptom for symptom, Mother had blurred the edge between his diseases and her own. His sigmoidoscopy was her sigmoidoscopy, and the prospect of going through it was making her jittery and defensive.

"I've never seen so many cars that are just people's cars around here," she said when we pulled into the hospital parking lot. We helped both parents unbend and get their weight over their feet. "You know, you can't count on the weather," she went on as we four tottered down a yellow-lit corridor, deeper into the bowels of an older wing. "It's usually just the weatherman's weather anyway." Instead of mauve and forest green, it was all dark wood, waxy tiles, and smoked glass. "Different people go to sleep in different ways," she reassured herself.

Dad and I crossed the threshold into the waiting room. We were marching as to war. Mother, on Cathy's arm, stopped short and surveyed the scene indignantly. "I'm not going to give in to this business," she said, beginning to hyperventilate. "You can't expect one little girl to fuck several lawyers."

When Dad's name was called, he was on his feet before I could help him, as if this were the moment he'd been waiting for, the promised vindication, the change in his fortunes, the cure—the moment he would step out of history, away from the four-inch thick medical file that included all the similar, inconclusive procedures performed on him in the past.

He answered the doctor's questions with simple yesses and nos, almost shyly, like a boy on a first date who yearned for intense conversation but had no idea how to make one start. I tried to add shading, detail, depth. I didn't want the excruciating pain that was causing regular crises in his life to change under interrogation into a minor discomfort.

I did want the interview to take longer, so Dad would feel satisfied that he had been heard. And I was trying to postpone the procedure itself, the embarrassment I anticipated for both him and me. Mother's pronouncements about his lack of shame couldn't have been farther from the mark—its currents had galvanized him for seventy years.

But Dad turned out to be no more self-conscious than a woman in childbirth—in the grips of a natural necessity. I stood at the head of the table with one arm around his shoulder, patting the flimsy fabric of his hospital gown, my other hand on his crisp hair.

I tried to imagine him young and strong, the man who'd let us children stand on his feet then twirled us in a dance, who'd helped us design science projects, solve math problems, parallel park. I couldn't. For some reason I recalled two bits of his advice, double suns that held my girl-life in sure orbit: "Always follow through on your commitments," and "If some kid asks you to do something you don't want to do, say your father won't let you, say I'm a mean ogre, and that's why you can't." I thought of stars collapsing, their light dying into private voids.

He didn't even know I was there.

❧

We had no reason to wonder what happened when those being cared for in a nursing home refused to cooperate with those giving care—when the caregiver felt all her good intentions thrown back in her face.

We had not hit that sort of impasse. For almost two years, love, humor, and a lot of fast talking had served to nudge our parents along whatever road we'd had to choose for them. If we'd slipped at times into benevolent dictating, it was to loosen an occasional benevolent balk.

"Mommy and I had a discussion last night," Dad would say to us.

"He's decided to go back to work," Mom would chime in. "He's going to send his application to EPA. He's willing to start at the bottom."

"I've got to get my driver's license renewed." Dad's plans often involved the restoration of his LTD.

But it never took much to tuck the two of them back into docility. They used to pride themselves on reasoning with us when we were kids; now we reasoned back. Why go to work when they had plenty of money, and commuting was a hassle, and Dad didn't know his way around Durham streets?

Then, one Saturday morning in September, Cathy and I rapped on their door and swung it open to find the liv-

ing room empty. When our hellos met with silence, we exchanged a puzzled glance, and for some reason approached
their bedroom door on tiptoe. What we saw made us freeze.

Dad sat in one corner in a straight chair, bent over so that
he could rest his forehead in one hand. He was wearing an
undershirt, boxers, and one dark blue sock. Mother was lying on his bed, a shirt of his twisted on over her slip, a brown
sock on one foot and two socks on the other, one brown and
one dark blue.

It was like stepping into distended time, the place of Dali
clocks, where it could take a day to get dressed, an hour to
process the sound of the word *Dad*.

When he finally lifted his head, he just stared at us,
speechless. It wasn't until Mother was awake and reaching
for more clothes that he emitted a word to acknowledge we
were there.

Meanwhile Cathy and I had started moving and chat-
tering very fast, suggesting the old stand-by, a trip to Duke
Gardens, sorting out the clothes they needed to put on, and
helping them into position to do so. The time it was taking
by then to get them into and out of the car would equal the
time we could spend actually stumbling along the pathways,
but gardens were our shrines; cameras, a mode of worship.
You could never refuse a call to behold the changing blooms
of a garden, to capture and hold them forever on film.

This time Dad did. Slowly he claimed he was too tired
and the day too muggy. Then he bowed his head again as if
fallen into a doze.

As we coaxed him, I picked up one of his hands and gave it a tug, idiotically saying, "You know you'll have a good time once you're there."

"For crying out loud, would you leave me alone?" he roared hoarsely. "Jesus Christ, what do I have to do to get you to lay off?"

I shrunk back, shocked to tears.

"Everybody's got to poke and push, poke and push."

Our mother looked at me knowingly. "That's the horror of finding a tragedy in your soup bowl," she said.

"I'm sorry," I told him, though I couldn't afford to realize what a bully I'd become.

"I'm going, I'm going," he said.

And then he did—it would be the last time—and Cathy set up some pictures in front of the flowers, which he snapped, and Mother's jazzed-up right brain recognized every stranger who crossed our path.

"See that couple up ahead of us," she said too loudly. "They're millionaires. If they want a garden named after them, they just pick up the phone."

More disabled, our father grew more stubborn, yet more disabled; he was losing the right to be stubborn at all. He bristled at all insults to his modesty, violations of his personal privacy, yet he could hardly do anything for himself.

Forward, sometimes flirtatious, the nursing assistants chafed his nerves. Maybe they commented on the sharpness of the clothes they were helping him put on, just as they were always telling Mother how pretty she looked. Maybe they actually turned to her and warned her to keep a close eye on a husband as handsome as hers. Maybe such remarks were what sparked her acute jealously, or at least fueled it. Who could guess what passed for innocuous chitchat? Sex: the lowest common denominator, the universal language. Everyone was speaking it except Dad.

One harmless misunderstanding he could never recover from: a playful nursing assistant passed him on the way to dinner and noticed that his fly was unzipped. What she said to him we will never know, though we felt certain she never intended her remark as ridicule. It was probably something like, "Careful there, General Best, you want to get us girls all riled up?"

When Chris arrived a few minutes later, he found Dad back in his room, refusing to eat. He was too mortified to explain clearly what happened, but Chris gathered that Dad felt he'd been accused of running around with his privates hanging out.

After that Dad froze whenever he saw that particular nursing assistant. More and more he sank into himself, refusing suggestions, treating outside help like an assault. We tried and sometimes succeeded in getting him to smile. But we understood the despair he must have been feeling, the fierce desire to be left alone.

In his position, we would have felt the same way. In our positions, helpless to offer comfort, we almost did.

The medical staff of Evergreen saw it differently, the medical staff which consisted of the full-time doctor in the

Wellness Center and whatever resident in geriatrics at Duke Hospital had been assigned to a brief rotation in Evergreen as a Fellow. To this medical staff, our father's problems were organic, not psychological. To them he was a dying body, not a distraught mind and wounded heart.

The medical staff was willing to admit that the boundaries weren't absolute and clear. But any treatment was. Our father was in the late stages of degenerative brain disease, exacerbated maybe by a urinary tract infection. Therefore, the staff doctor would take another look at his meds, and put him on an antibiotic just in case.

So much for our father's dispirited spirit. If he was becoming more and more uncooperative, there could be only one reason: the chemistry of cooperation was out of whack. He was agitated, and *agitation*, that catch-all crime of the very old, took a simple chemical fix.

We never guessed what was coming. What did we know about care of the elderly? At some point we must have read Evergreen's written pledge about the administration of its assisted living facility and its nursing home. No physical restraints, it promised, and we missed the subtext.

Because what did physical restraints have to do with getting our frail parents clothed and fed, their medications reliably doled, in a pleasant, protected environment? What did physical restraints have to do with life at the end of the twentieth century, for that matter? Evergreen might as well have been boasting that they no longer applied leeches to a sick patient's neck.

It never occurred to us that if a nursing facility abjured physical restraints, they might turn to something worse.

If the facility also denied its residents any psychological dimension, from the refinements of emotion to the newborn's drive for pleasure over pain, so that soothing words, song and dance, bribes, or a temporary backing off had nowhere to register—if the resident's mind, in other words, had been proclaimed an unreceptive blank—the recourse became chemical restraints, injected sedatives such as Haldol or Mellaril, with problematic side effects like hallucinations.

ళ్ళ

Our father had literally raised cane.

We guessed he was trying to ward off all the people he didn't want to see, the suggestions he didn't want to hear. We guessed that in his mind he was in full uniform, defending his bunker against great odds.

The medical staff disagreed. He was beyond wanting. There was no question of a mind. It was just the disease, which made him not only uncooperative, but also *agitated*, a threat to himself and others.

A dangerous man, even though in his advanced stage of Parkinson's, he moved his body with great difficulty, and excruciating slowness. Dangerous even though he was tractable enough to allow a staff member in close enough to administer an injection that would render him safe.

Haldol and Mellaril do not prevent episodes of agitation, and in Dad's case, they wound up creating a backlash of hallucinations worse than the episodes themselves. Since state regulations fortunately forbade giving a patient a second shot too soon after the first, the staff finally called Chris, who sped over, and with quiet talk and gentle touch, calmed our father down.

Afterwards, he confronted the nurse and insisted the injections not be used again. They were introducing randomly timed bursts of powerful chemicals into his system, where the life-critical balance of Eldepril and Synemet, along with Zoloft and Synthroid, could be too easily upset.

Chris's insistence was the executive director's cue. It was time to move our parents down one level to Pine Center, the nursing home. There the staff-patient ratio would allow more creative solutions to our father's *agitation*. They would both get the attention they needed, expectations would be lower, they would be safer, *et cetera*.

The doctor cited a last piece of evidence—it was a little story he told us to prove how far gone our father really was. It took place in the bedroom of our parents' suite, where he and his Fellow from Duke had allegedly come to check reports of our father's *agitation*. They tried to talk to him about moving to Pine Center below. The subject did indeed agitate him—so much that he undid his fly, pulled out his penis, and urinated on the mauve and forest green tweed carpet.

So an old man for whom simple reflexes—the lift of a fork, a greeting—took long minutes, a man who could no longer manage buckles, buttons, zippers, and who, incidentally, according to them lacked the cognitive complexity to

feel defiance—this old man, we were told, managed a significantly defiant gesture so suddenly and adeptly that two
young men could only stand by and watch.

We were exhausted, Chris particularly, who by now had
been called in two more times to pick up the pieces of our
chemically blown-apart father and put them back together
again. But how could we give up our duty, our promises, our
own story, the one that ended happily?

Our parents were hardly bed-ridden, and we knew the
dread they harbored of the nursing home at the bottom of
the elevator. We knew they had minds enough to feel that
we'd consigned them to a fate worse than death. On top of
that, the executive director refused to cut another door, and
we worried about the trauma of separating them after fifty
years of sleeping in the same room.

We attended a meeting: the anointed Fellow from Duke;
the director of Pine, a woman with a Master's in Fine Arts
and whose experience with the elderly consisted of handling
PR for the Governor's committee on aging; the nutritionist;
a nurse; Cathy, Chris, and myself.

The director of Pine described a special Alzheimer's wing
they were planning downstairs, for residents such as our parents who were still ambulatory. It would open on a garden,
where they could walk safely and sit on benches and enjoy the
flowers. Eventually the garden might even shelter rabbits and
ducks for the residents to pet. The plans had been drafted by
one of Durham's top landscape architects, they were already
finalized, their execution was set for the near future.

We had lost our taste for resistance. Besides, the director of Pine had uttered magic, disarming words. How could
a Best say no to a garden, or to the *near future*? We didn't
question the practicality of the animals, like where they were
going to go to the bathroom and how they would be kept
from eating the vegetation. All at once we realized that what
was happening was what we'd known all along would have to
happen. And we could let it happen without a fight.

⌒ 6 ⌒

THE VORTEX

The beautiful things could make you laugh, each one like a familiar word repeated, repeated, until all its useful meaning had been peeled away and it was just there, an oddity, an arbitrary arrangement of sound.

Bone china. Bone china.

Why did they call it bone, when it was nothing so enduring, more like pale, tattooed flesh?

"I want you to have that someday," our mother said to each of us about one beautiful thing or another, back when our notion of death was more clear-cut and tidy, conventional. Not this—the five of us groping a path through the debris.

No one could meet anyone else's eyes. Pool truths, and we would drown.

Tragedy in a soup bowl, indeed.

The floor-plan of Pine—two corridors laid out in a cross—was enough like the floor-plan upstairs in Spruce to deceive Mother. She seemed finally to conclude that it wasn't she who had moved, but everything else. Our father's room was now across the hall from hers, and the sweet-smelling but never-used communal parlor in Spruce, with its chintz-covered sofas, had been made over to accommodate a fan of reclining wheelchairs centered on a droning TV. The nurses' station, which used to be a little counter off to one side, had been expanded and now sprawled large as a hospital's at the center where the two corridors intersected.

But the dining room had been left the same, and our parents' table still occupied the same spot. And in her room, the same flowered curtains framed the same window looking out on the same lawn, kindly raised now to eye level. Desperate for good news, we told her about the garden they were planning to put in right outside. She said she already knew all about it, and it was either going to sink or swim.

Dad could see the difference. When we pointed out his room, he pressed his lips together and advanced his lower jaw. Chris was hoping maybe there would turn out to be benefits in separating our parents. Maybe Dad's constant presence inspired Mother's wild jealousy, which in turn goaded his agitation. "I don't know," was all Dad would say now. "I don't know."

He had not missed the fact that the staff in Pine included two male nursing assistants, one of whom was over six feet tall and weighed about 250 pounds. When the latter intro-

duced himself, Dad turned away. Later, he referred to the
man as *the Cop*.

Cathy and I first felt the difference at dinnertime, having
scooted up to the cafeteria for our usual trays of food. We
were helping our parents remove the lids from their various
dishes when a nursing assistant positioned two very old wom-
en in reclining wheelchairs at the table next to us and un-
covered plates holding scoops of something beige, something
pale green, and something white. Then with gentle efficiency
the aide pried open the soft, old mouths with loaded spoons
and slipped the contents inside. Sometimes the puree came
out again, and sometimes there was coughing that sounded fatal. The rhythm of feeding would break, then resume.
Meanwhile at a second table a woman tried to eat her apple
juice with a fork while another consumed her meal, mashed
potatoes and all, with her hands.

All around us the clearly partitioned surface of each tray
became expressionistic. Half a canned peach and a nibbled
chicken breast swam in spilled milk. Frozen yogurt adorned
a little dish of string beans. I thought of my daughter, who
never wanted "things touching other things" on her plate. "It
all goes to the same place," I used to say, as I had been told.
But Cathy and I would not try to take our meals in the dining room again.

The room next door to our father's belonged to Paul,
who was almost ninety. Five and a half feet tall with white
hair down to his shoulders, his wizened face a patchwork of
stubble, he hobbled around poking an untrimmed fingernail

at the female staff members and visitors, chortling, "You're certainly a cute one." They generally replied that he was cute too. What he was was an *easy* one, perfectly content to wear a sweat suit with pull-on pants.

Dad didn't own a sweat suit. You might as well be walking around in your pajamas as a sweatshirt, if you asked him. He had not yet figured out that sweat suits made things much easier once you were wearing Depends.

Cathy and I left our parents sitting stiffly in Mom's room, where a large TV was mounted on the wall just high enough regularly to bump your head. We'd turned it on, though neither of them showed any interest in watching it, then struggled to detach and head back north.

❧

A week later Chris called to report trouble with Dad. It was that Evergreen word again: *agitation*. Superficial, emotionless. A word for washing machines and cement mixers, for roused rabble. A word that categorically denied anger, embarrassment, fear.

Had a staff member tried to put a diaper on our father, or give him a shower? Private baths were no longer attached to each room. According to a master schedule, residents were taken down the hall in robe and slippers to a bathing room.

As far as the medical staff was concerned, the agitation was unprovoked, unmotivated. Dad simply flailed at a nurse with his cane and hit her. She took his cane away and gave him an injection of Haldol, escalating the cycle of distress.

Last resorts first again: knock him into outer space, then phone Chris to reel him back in.

Chris had been over to sit with Dad, and as he tried to talk him down, our father had shared a garbled account of being a hazing victim back in college, when his trousers were removed and he'd been rolled up in a rug.

Memory, or delusion?

Or the more pertinent question: human emotion or mere *agitation*, along the lines of a daddy-longlegs when you pull off one leg?

They tried antibiotics for a urinary tract or any other infection. They tried Haldol again, despite our outcries and promises from the Fellow from Duke that he would cancel doctor's orders for the drug "as needed." We began to wonder if we had bumped up against something sacred in the culture of nursing homes, like the right some think inalienable of a parent to spank his child.

The Fellow from Duke, nearing the end of his six-month rotation at Evergreen, came up with a bright idea. Maybe it was a negative interaction among our father's medications that was causing such unmanageable behavior. Then for some reason, without consulting us, the staff doctor gave the go-ahead for this apprentice in geriatrics to experiment. He withheld one of the two Parkinson's drugs Dad had been taking for ten years.

This move did change our father's behavior. Within two days his body had locked in a rigid palsy. He was verging on comatose. He had to be carried between bed and chair, his body forced to the contours of each. He stopped being able to eat or to open his mouth wide enough to be fed.

He became a paradox: paralyzed yet finally, undeniably, relentlessly *agitated.*

During this period of frozen trembling, sure enough, the nurse he had whacked with his cane entered an episode of *agitation* in his medical record, along with the shot of Haldol she administered to punish it.

We should have been used to it, being caught by surprise, being too late, scrambling and grasping as our parents' fate was sucked out of our hands: The Vortex, and we'd come to know it by a whine in the ears, the immeasurable difference in pressure between death looming closer and our intentions.

Cathy and I flew down from DC, rushed to his bedside, which had become a mattress on the floor. If the agitation the medical staff had finally produced should jerk him right out of bed, he wouldn't have far to fall. If we'd entered that room a dozen times and found our father that changed, the horror and pain would have been just as raw on the thirteenth.

His eyes were half shut, but we thought we saw a blink of recognition, a flustered stab at speech.

It hit like a fist to the belly, the truth that he was finished, over the edge—there was no dragging him back.

We had failed to protect him, failed to block the madness in Evergreen's methods. We were worthless.

A nurse attempted to comfort Cathy and me. She looked as stricken as we were. Chris's wife Lisa knelt on the floor trying to feed our father dissolved Synemet, the cancelled medication, with a spoon. In disbelief, Chris recalled the pleasant time they'd had with our parents at Christmas, a little over a week before—later he would show us photographs of them smiling up into the camera, a grandchild on either side.

Hunching on the periphery, Mother seemed to know this was it. Upstairs in Spruce, she'd told us that she and Dad had discussed death, and he'd admitted he was afraid, but she'd told him there wasn't anything to be afraid of.

Less sure now what to do and with the air of someone being watched, she stumbled over to the head of his mattress to deliver a little speech: "I'm sorry you're feeling sick, sweetheart. Try to get well. I'll be right next door." Then she shuffled out.

The Fellow from Duke put his head in the door like someone expecting a grenade. When we joined him out in the hallway, he offered his opinion. Our father's meds were acting up, this could happen in cases of Parkinson's, the combination that worked for years could suddenly stop working. He, personally, was very sorry this had happened. They were still doing everything they could to stabilize him. But patients with Parkinson's do eventually succumb to the disease, he reminded us. There was no cure.

It was as if he spoke a foreign language, uninflected, impoverished. For us to compose questions in it would have taken too much effort, and they would never have gotten us to the heart of things anyway. Whatever that was, the heart of things. *This old man is still a human being like the rest of us. My patient, my father, myself.*

At dinnertime the Cop came in, greeted us heartily and set down a tray of food—a plate of pork chops, mashed potatoes, and peas; tossed salad; a piece of cake. He bent over our father, poked his hands under his armpits, lifted, and swung him into the easy chair situated near the foot of the mattress.

"Wait a minute," I said, but not forcefully enough to call a halt to the maneuver. Against all evidence, I was still trying stupidly to believe that a staff member might know what he was doing.

Just then Dad's face twisted and he let out a loud cry. But it was all too late—he now sat slumped in the chair, gasping and groaning softly. His eyes were still at half-mast.

The Cop carved off a chunk of meat and touched it to Dad's lips, which clenched. "He ate a good lunch," the Cop told us. Against all evidence.

"You can go," we said to him. "We'll help him with this." He left.

Mother wandered in. "It's Molly and Cathy, Bill," she said. "You know. Your two precious girls. You've got to eat something, dear."

Neither Cathy nor I bothered to reach for the fork.

By the next morning, Sunday, his color had faded completely, his breathing consisted of shuddering snores. There was something around his parched mouth that looked like dried blood. A rotund, grey-haired LPN, eyes wide with authority, speculated that he might have been trying to eat his feces. As I tried to bring my weeping under control enough to focus on her, she added vaguely, "They do that, you know."

The staff was in a state of panic. One more new thing we had to learn: nursing homes strongly prefer that their residents die quietly during the night shift. It is difficult for the nurses and assistants to witness physical suffering and not be able to do anything to make it go away. What they wanted to do with Dad was call an ambulance and send him to the emergency room at Duke Hospital.

Reluctant to drag him out into winter weather, and maybe greater chaos, we got them to call the Fellow from Duke instead. After all, he'd said we could. If there was anything more he could do.

We suspected our father was dehydrated, we told him over the phone. Hence the parched scabs in his mouth. How could he, semi-conscious, have taken in much of anything the last couple days?

Well, there was a problem with ordering an IV, said the Fellow from Duke. The nursing home wasn't really equipped to hook our father to one. That procedure required a hospital.

The next thing we knew, Dad was being strapped to a stretcher. He struggled and grimaced in weak bursts, then subsided into whimpering. Cathy and I cried with him, for him, as they loaded him into the back of the ambulance. We had to ride up front beside the driver. "Please," we say, "no need for a siren." We cried harder when he agreed.

Cathy and I were sitting in a little room with the Fellow from Duke, who wanted to discuss his cutting-edge view on dying. He reassured us that he didn't believe in prolonging suffering by means of heroic measures. He was proud to be the sort of doctor who had the humility not to resort to them. "So are we all on the same page?" he wanted to know. "Comfort measures only? Death with dignity?"

Finally allowed into the examining room, Cathy and I took stands on either side of Dad's stretcher. X-rays had revealed fractured ribs, thanks to the Cop. A nurse tried to hook up an IV to rehydrate him for one last round, but his jerking tremor sabotaged her efforts. She began taping down his arms. So there they finally were, the physical restraints.

Our father managed a burst of weak resistance that threatened to tangle everything. I mustered a quick, stern, "Now stop that, Dad, we've got to do this." And briefly he opened his eyes and seemed to focus on Cathy and me.

"You've always had such pretty eyes," Cathy said, and his face relaxed in a smile.

More tears from me, gushing up from the depths of good-bye. How could we all be suffering so and still nothing be getting done right?

The nurse patted my hand. "It's OK. Don't you worry," she said. "We're going to take good care of your dad."

He lived for one more week, back in his room in Pine, stretched out on a whole bed, cranked high off the floor, head raised, guard rails in place. He'd been stilled by fever, pneumonia. When they'd brought him back from the hospital that Sunday, rehydrated but still comatose, someone had pressed him to try a bite of food—pork chop? tossed salad?—

and he inhaled it instead. Finally we were not surprised.

Think of it as assisted suicide, we told each other, squinting against that whirling wind. Our father had stumbled into the sort of *no-win situation* he'd always warned us to avoid. The nutritionist who kept sending down the trays of inedible food, the nurse with the Haldol, the staff doctor and his Fellow from Duke with the bright idea—all became the witless accomplices in his decision to end a life whose quality had sunk below zero. We waited for the moment that would set him free.

His eyes were shut, his mouth dropped open, chalk dry. His lungs sucking in air expelled a different smell, cheesy sour—the room filled with it. Clenched in one fist was a leather pouch containing a polished blue stone. His eyes streaming with rare tears, Chris had tucked it there, a Native-American custom he'd heard about. The stone offered our father's spirit a new place to reside.

Cathy and I took turns trying to talk to that spirit now. We told our father how much he meant to us, how grateful we'd been for his guidance and concern. We apologized for the insanity, the hell he'd been through, and tried to assure him that what awaited him would bring relief from it, peace. Maybe we faltered in our promises. How did we know, after all, what awaited him?

But then the staff doctor poked his face around the half-open door, doleful, a study in compassion, and we realized our promises were all safe to make. What lay ahead for him had to be better than this.

The doctor knew just how we felt because he recently lost his mother. As though bearing good news, he predicted that it wouldn't be long now for our father, then added, like a bonus, that he was willing to prescribe morphine, to guarantee that our father felt no discomfort and perhaps to speed the process of dying. He was checking for himself—were we all on the same page?

We supposed we were. Alternative pages were worse and there was no closing the book yet.

For some reason then, standing only a few feet from our father, the doctor began to describe the death rattle. Appalled, we waved him silent. He shrugged—still refusing to be scientific, were we? Still unable to comprehend that if several weeks ago our father was too far gone to have feelings, we certainly didn't have to worry about him now?

Mother drifted in like a child out of sorts, wanting something but unable to say what. "Are you going to join us for supper?" she asked her dying husband. "You can't lie down forever." Then she changed her mind. "Or maybe you can."

"Dad's going to be all right," we told her. "He's suffered for a long time but now he's dying. He will be at peace."

"I know that," she said. "If we can only keep that show on the slope."

Why didn't we sing to him, Cathy and I suggested, and we broke into a medley of the songs he'd taught us, a lifetime ago, to accompany those inevitable road-trips in the station wagon: "It Ain't Gonna Rain No More," "I've Been Working on the Railroad," "Take Me Out to the Ballgame." Mother

followed along, chiming in every few words. When we were
finished, there was a long silence.

Then Mother's flat soprano rose to a song she and Dad
used to croon as a duet, while we kids gagged and rolled our
eyes at their mushiness. It must have been a popular ballad
that summer the two of them met as teenagers in the Poconos. Retrieving it from some still undamaged pocket of her
brain, she sang it now all by herself.

There's a long, long trail a-winding
Unto the land of my dreams,
Where the nightingale is singing
And the pale moon gleams.

We helped with the second verse, humming past blanks,
hitting the last line in unison.

There's a long, long time a-waiting
Until my dreams all come true,
Till the day that I'll be winding
Down that long, long trail with you.

In the end, Dad played his approved role. He lay motion-
less for several days, in no apparent discomfort, making only
the noise of congested breathing. With the flesh of his face
melted down to bone, he might even have been said to possess dignity. Then in the early hours of one morning when no
one was with him, he died.

It happened during the shift of a nurse who seemed as
sad to lose him as we were. She'd never had problems with

him, she told us, never had to resort to Haldol, even inti-
mated that during those last weeks what went on with him
had not been right.

Before calling us around 3:00 A.M., she'd washed and
dressed his body, combed its hair. Now Chris, Cathy, and
I each spent a few minutes alone with it, bidding good-bye.

A doctor we'd never seen before signed the death cer-
tificate, and a call was put in to the cremation service with
which Cathy had made prior arrangements.

Instantly, it seemed, a young man with smooth cheeks
and pale, smooth hair was manipulating a stretcher through
Pine's door. When we registered surprise at his speedy appearance, he told us that his job was to cruise the streets of
Durham all night in his unmarked van, waiting for calls like
ours. Other young men did the same during the day.

That many people die.

We wrapped our father's body in his special blanket, last
in the long line that had been his secret sources of security
since we'd been old enough to notice.

Something we didn't do, which was not right: we couldn't
face waking up our mother. We claimed exhaustion. Why
ask for trouble? we were thinking. We slipped into the emotional cowardice we had come to hate in the doctors. We
denied her heart.

~ 7 ~

THE CRACKS OF TIME

I opened my eyes to find her hovering, hands clasped prayer-like over her breastbone, asking, "Did you see my little boy, a dark-haired you?"

I snapped out of a strangely euphoric dream—Dad reassuring me everything would turn out fine—and remembered where I was—dozing in one of Pine's unoccupied rooms, waiting to take care of our mother as soon as she awoke.

I put my arms around her rounded shoulders, blurting, "Dad died during the night, sweetie. He is finally at peace. Finally free. Everything's going to be all right. They've taken his body away to be cremated, which is what he wanted."

Fast talk, and too loud, stacking up truths to block the dawning error it was too late to correct.

Always *too late.* After a few hours sleep, the comfort of a dream, I couldn't believe we hadn't allowed her to say good-bye to him. *Human beings can only stand so much reality*, I thought. That may be, but it's not as if there *is* anything else.

"I don't know what the story is," Mother said. "But it's nothing criminal. I have no trouble with girls, and boys can just get out of the way."

Arm in arm, we inched back down the hall to her room. She tugged me in the direction of Dad's, and we stopped for some minutes in the open doorway, taking in the vacancy.

"How are you feeling?" I finally asked.

"I'm trying to think of whom I'm burying," she said. "He was just a little bit behind themselves, I was thinking to myself as I slept here. It will be a difficult journey."

"Yes, it has been. I'm sorry," I said, one more time. It seemed to be all I could ever say.

"It's not your fault," she said automatically.

"We could have done better. Hopefully it'll be a little easier now that Dad's blazed the trail."

She met my eyes gamely, her brow furrowed, but around her mouth the hint of a smile. It was a look we would see often in the coming weeks: earnest, yet prepared to laugh at herself if what she said turned out to be a joke. "It's time to ward off evil," she said, "and bring in god."

She cried mildly in bursts as she sorted through the stacks of condolence cards and something someone wrote stirred the loss.

Yet she was easily distracted. One staff member paged another on the intercom. A resident down the hall started screaming *shit, shit*. Her next-door neighbor wandered into her room laughing and muttering. And Mother would perk up like a gossip with access to a couple of party lines and forget grief.

What made her more sad and anxious than Dad's death was our anger over it. He had been in stable condition in Spruce. Three weeks downstairs in Pine and he was dead. Since when was *agitation* a capital offense?

We were writing letters, calling state regulatory agencies, meeting with the Evergreen staff doctor, and generally feeling outraged that drugs like Haldol could be injected at whim into old, failing bodies.

A patient advocacy group in Washington, DC, decried the practice, and individual doctors we talked to privately shook their heads. The outside physician at Duke Hospital who had been treating our father's Parkinson's called it madness when Chris had consulted him after the first two episodes, but he never picked up the phone to challenge his colleague at Evergreen, and matter now for deep regret, we were too polite to pressure him.

Behind his desk in the Wellness Clinic, the Evergreen doctor reminded me that the drugs were altogether legal, and swore to keep them in his *arsenal*. His professional compassion narrowed to a squint when he added, "If you're not satisfied with the approach here, you are certainly welcome to move your mother to another facility. Then you might be surprised to find out how really primitive conditions can be."

Evergreen's were primitive enough for Chris, who reported his daily visits with bitter resignation: "This is it, rock bottom. One flew over the cuckoo's nest. People screaming at all hours, walking around wearing their underpants for a hat." When he, Cathy, and I were together, we had nothing but snide remarks for Evergreen's administration.

Mom didn't like all the undercurrents. "Now, be nice," she'd chide. She said she liked the Evergreen doctor. "He's twenty-four years old and he makes his own chowder."

Maybe she understood the politics of dependency and reprisal. Maybe she sensed, as eventually we all would, that Pine wouldn't be quite as dangerous a place for her.

You couldn't miss her.

Dazzling in a brand new, bright red dress with gold buttons, and huge gold-tone earrings, she had been tucked into a rose-colored vinyl wing chair out by the nurses' station.

She looked up when we called *Mother*, a hint of mischief in her bright red, lipsticked smile. Some of the lipstick was on her upper front teeth, along with whatever she'd eaten for breakfast. Her naturally wavy hair was slicked back with mousse like a Spanish dancer's. She was a new woman.

"How are you doing?" we asked.

"I'm getting great at collecting quiet," she said.

Betraying everything she had ever taught us about feminine artifice, we told her she looked beautiful. Her eyes twinkled. She thought she did.

She showed us her fingernails, which we remembered as never polished, always carefully filed, but often dark-rimmed with indelible garden soil. They were longer now, and bright red. Privately we were a little appalled.

"Have I made the acquaintance of you ladies?" A round face peeked around the flange of the adjacent wing chair.

"We're Evelyn's daughters," we answered. "And who are you?" we asked.

"He's the new boy," Mom said.

"Herman Mandelbaum," said the man. "Professor of languages at Harvard University."

"Oh, really," we said, "that's very impressive. Which languages would those be?"

"The spoken ones," he said. "Is this your mother?" He was sitting on the edge of his chair now, gripping his walker, as if ready to leap to his feet. We nodded. "Is she vigorous?" he wanted to know.

Mom giggled and rolled her eyes our way—*see what she had to put up with?*

"We think she is," we said. "We're taking her out to lunch. Watch this." Mother grasped Cathy's extended hands, and Cathy tugged her up out of the chair.

"Good idea," Professor Mandelbaum said.

As we moved away, he was lurching his walker around to his other side, where a woman with rippling, shoulder-length, platinum hair sat in a wheelchair. She wore her makeup comfortably, like an aged movie star, along with a flowered muumuu and a quiet smile on her perfect face.

"Allow me to introduce myself," he said.

The woman gazed at him, the quiet smile unchanged.

"Herman Mandelbaum of Harvard University," he said, leaning at her over his walker.

She kept smiling.

☙

When we asked Mother if she'd settled in yet to her new room, she told us it was a popular watering hole, and always would be, as long as we continued to have such spacious rains. We understood her clearly to mean that she was comfortable, yet she added, "I'm beginning to talk in a crazy language."

"Don't you worry," we said. "It isn't crazy to us."

We could never believe her addled brain was simply making an addled noise. Even near the end of her life, when she was hardly able to move or open her mouth wide enough for her pureed food, when she would begin to have difficulty swallowing it—even when her scrambled speech would trail off into silence—surprisingly clear apologies for her own condition would rise out of the chaos to startle us: "When you get a good idea, it goes right downstairs."

For Chris, the crazy language was still something to endure, a sad reminder that he'd lost her. She seemed to save her complaining for him, about other residents, the ubiquitous cats, about being publicly shamed for stealing things when she hadn't. Every dinner hour he stopped in to check on her, weathering her moodiness and her oracular nonsense, and cutting up the hunk of chop or chicken breast on her plate. As he saw it, his job now was to shield her from the greater insanity that was Evergreen's administration—the folks who had killed our father. He sent notes to the nutritionist, suggesting more user-friendly recipes for Pine residents, but big, stubborn hunks of meat kept being sent down to be poked at and left uneaten on the trays.

Cathy and I had it a lot easier. We were the pleasant surprise, the break in routine. One weekend a month we could be all patience and affection. One weekend a month, she could talk and talk, a sort of agitation of the mouth. And we could refuse to believe it was just the spasms of disease, random firings: for us she was spinning the world according to Evelyn—a poem to interpret, a dream to decode.

Into her second month in Pine, Mother decided she'd been hired to take care of the other residents because she'd always had a way with the poor.

She introduced us to Betty, her next-door neighbor. Betty was a laugher. Laughing must have felt more natural that the effort to talk, which produced only a mishmash of inflected syllables. If we pretended to understand the syllables—we almost thought we did—she would laugh and laugh.

Her eyes were dark and deep-set under rather undisciplined eyebrows. For some reason no one had tried to beautify her, maybe because she still *was* very vigorous, marching up and down the hall in an oddly perky outfit for February—flowered Bermudas and a shirt with a flower appliqué to match—hugging herself as if she was cold.

"Don't touch her food," Mother warned us, and Chris confirmed: the last thing you wanted to do was offer to cut her meat. She'd growl and bare her teeth.

Lorraine also paced the hall in a prim shirtwaist, her hair neatly coiffed, asking with increasing urgency after her husband. "Where's P. J.? Where's P. J.?"

Once we saw Mother grab Lorraine's arm, stopping her. "P. J. is coming. You know P. J. cares about you, and he'll be here as soon as he can." She had spoken the truth, and she looked as surprised as Lorraine did, who trundled quietly back to her room.

Mrs. Schipp, in her late eighties, was the problem child, Mother told us, a very bad girl. But what could you expect of the child of a vagrant who'd been pushed from an airplane?

On the door of Mrs. Schipp's room hung a photograph of a middle-aged woman, dignified in her bubble hair-do and flowered blouse with floppy bow. But curled into her wheelchair now, she *was* child-sized, and if you moved her or tried to help her in any way, she lashed out with bionic pinches and a barrage of curses you couldn't imagine the bubble-haired lady had ever known. Her ranting became a sort of background music in Pine.

Sometimes one of her tantrums stopped so suddenly that we suspected Haldol. Then we'd find her asleep at the nurses' station, her head bowed to her knees.

Having been pinched once too often, Mother steered clear of her. But Mrs. Schipp was "good with children," she conceded. "And if you tell her it's chicken, she eats."

Sure enough, that afternoon brought a parade of Schipps, three generations to visit the woman in the photograph: a daughter bearing a gift-box of Kentucky Fried, two granddaughters, each with a great-granddaughter, one pulled by the wrist, the other in arms.

Mrs. Schipp was handed the baby. Cathy and I held our breath, but she cradled it like a pro. The toddler hung on the wheelchair and obediently gave great-grandma a kiss on the arm. Mrs. Schipp's eyes had widened and focused. Her face, usually furrowed in a sulk, opened in a radiant smile.

At dinner Betty sat by herself, chin low over her plate. Lorraine and P. J. shared a table. Now that her husband had appeared, she ignored him and his entreaties that she eat. She just stared straight ahead with round, milky eyes.

Cathy and I sat with Mom at the larger round table in the center. Mrs. Schipp was on one side of me, clutching a crispy drumstick. I asked her if it tasted good.

"Hunh?" she asked indignantly.

I repeated the question.

"Hunh?" she asked again.

Across from us a nursing assistant spooned mush into the mouth of a woman whose gaze and expression were blank. The only muscles that still moved were in her throat.

The chair on Cathy's other side awaited a feisty woman introduced as Emma. Stout and bow-legged, she'd lurched into the dining room behind her walker wearing a half-slip over her sweats.

Emma was no-frills blunt, even combative. Earlier that day we'd heard her deflect Professor Mandelbaum's gallantries: "I do not care to make your acquaintance. I do not care if you get lost. You're none of your own business."

"I'm glad to see you, Emma," Cathy said when she'd adjusted herself on the chair. "I was wondering where you were." Emma melted into sweet and demure.

Across the room, the Professor ogled Serena, the woman with the platinum tresses, whose smug, mysterious smile seemed completely appropriate. She managed to preserve it and her allure even though eating with her hands.

At the last table slouched a thin, striking woman in off-white slacks and sweater which matched her off-white, well-cut straight hair. Her eyebrows arched like slim, white boomerangs. She was ignoring the monolithic meat on her plate in favor of the more chewable pink carnation in the central vase. Cathy leaned closer as she cut our mother's veal, cocked her head in the woman's direction, asked, "Who's that?"

"They can't saddle me with her too," Mother replied.

Later we scouted the corridors and found out that Mary Beach, a new resident, was that creature whom our mother had always envied and scorned—a Socialite. In the photograph on her door, we saw a beautiful woman in a ball gown caught in mid-twirl, flinging a flirtatious glance over one bare shoulder. The bio underneath spoke of charities, a symphony orchestra association.

We also learned what we could have guessed, that the man who'd sat beside her on a motorized cart was her husband. He came down from Spruce to dine with Mary, who didn't quite make the grade upstairs.

He rebuked her for eating the flower, and for sticking her knife in her milk, and for interrupting the meal to remove

her knee-high hose, which became her consuming mission—
to roll up the legs of her off-white pants and roll down her
stockings. He would never give up. For the louder he scolded
her, the more capable and normal he felt.

All those faces, half-framed by white bibs—each month
they would grow more familiar. All those lives running out,
energies winding down, slipping through the cracks of time
into something else.

It would happen sooner rather than later to Mrs. Schipp,
to Paul, and to Herman Mandelbaum. Cathy and I would
arrive for our visit and their rooms would be emptied out,
just as our father's had been. They would finally become the
people they had once been, the enlarged images hanging on
each door. The doting mother, the irresistible charmer, the
professor of languages, the individuals their families could
remember.

Forgotten would be the people they were now.

We were chatting with the nursing assistant across from
us as she fed her charge. She asked us how old we were and
we told her "over fifty."

"You should keep that a secret," the young woman said
tactfully. "Nobody would ever know."

In her corner of the room, Mary Beach stopped fiddling
with her stockings. White brows rose into an expression of
haughty forbearance. "I don't think so," she said. "Someone's
got to put out the word."

8

NO CLEAN ESCAPE

The masks had been peeled away. Impatient mother. Passive-aggressive wife. Perennial outsider, suspicious and critical. Woman besieged by fear.

All those past selves had vanished. Maybe they'd died with our father. Maybe Chris had banished them by refusing to listen when she complained of persecution. Maybe Cathy and I had exorcised them by encouraging the details of her wildest dreams until she lost interest in them herself. Or was it just that the brain-plaque of Alzheimer's had clogged the machinery of neurosis along with everything else, filled in the ragged, badly meshing grooves?

Chris didn't feel the alteration as much as Cathy and I did. He had been her baby. He'd had the best of her, and now, with the duty of daily oversight, he had if not the worst, at least the most difficult. But to Cathy and me, "the girls" she'd criticized and demeaned, whose needs had struck her as intolerable—to us, the change seemed almost miraculous.

She became the perfect patient, amenable and constantly grateful. She couldn't praise Chris's attentions enough, though half the time she called him Bill, nor did she tire of telling Cathy and me how much she loved us. We'd had to give up on phone calls because she tended to put the receiver down in mid-"conversation" and wander off, but whenever we appeared before her, her dazed expression broke into a grin and she gathered her energy to fill us in on all the news.

The brothel she had staunchly condemned had become a school. She was studying Latin America, she was about to graduate *magna cum laude*, Betty had gotten herself pregnant, Mrs. Schipp had been expelled (having died quietly one night). "Yesterday we glued little pictures on and sprayed them. Later we're going to eat them."

"Pictures of what?" I asked.

"A chemist, a baby, and a rubber hose. This is a hopping town," she added, by way of summary. "One of those places with peanut shells."

For our father it had been confinement. He became a POW sworn to escape if it killed him. But for her, it was as if such straitened space felt finally safe.

Maybe in that friendly, appealing woman we were glimpsing the real, true Evelyn, the original spirit stripped of life's accidents, encrustations like our father and us four kids.

In Pine she was fussed over like a queen, hair, makeup, nails, clothes, pills and more pills. She didn't have to go to anyone; everyone came to her. She spoke and people were mystified, delighted, entertained.

A nurse approached with a little cup of tablets. "Hello, Mrs. Best, what do you think I've got here?"

"Three coins in the window," Mother suggested, her face expectant, hopeful—would we get her joke?

"That's right. It's that time again."

"These are the times men's toes are stole," quipped Mother with a droll smile.

If the anger and pain over our father's death were subsiding, it was because Mother's mellow grace had seduced us. Even Chris began to concede that there was more to Pine than its bumbling policies. The facility had been brand new when we arrived, after all. There were kinks in the system. The executive director, for one, with no prior experience in geriatric care or nursing home administration. The director of Pine, for another, with no prior experience in geriatric care or nursing home administration. In time shouldn't their on-the-job learning curve wobble up from its zero-axis?

The nurse who'd shared our horror at our father's fate had resigned and dropped from sight, but so too had the Cop whom we'd watch fracture Dad's ribs. And the nurse who loved Haldol quit to have a baby. Most important, instead of the phalanx of temporary nurses and aides, who couldn't tell you anything or do anything because they were just temps, a core of permanent staff had begun to form, hanging onto their positions despite the low pay and demanding, unpredictable schedules. Eventually their good faith and spunk, patience and common sense created an atmosphere in Pine that had little to do with what went on in the administrative offices upstairs.

Upstairs the administration kept busy putting out a monthly newsletter on pretty paper, which toted up all the on-paper commendations of Pine. Upstairs they negotiated a change in the pharmaceutical provider, to one that delivered patient medications in premeasured doses and charged twice as much.

Upstairs they decided that what the patients in Pine really needed were bracelets that activated a siren if they crossed the threshold to the outside. These devices would back up the number-pad installed beside the single door, which required the punching of a three-digit code to release the lock.

Chris phoned the administration upstairs. He got them to acknowledge that except in a case as rare as the roomful of monkeys typing *Hamlet*, no patient in Pine could manage to key in the sequence, which was changed regularly. Their concern, however, was that some patient might manage to scoot out the door after it had been opened by someone else, when the someone else wasn't looking. The bracelets would cost an additional monthly fee.

Chris absolutely refused to pay it. Our mother was barely able to walk with support, he pointed out.

Our case would be discussed, he was told.

Cathy and I were sitting in Mother's room having one of those meandering chats we'd come to enjoy when we heard a slap-clunk, slap-clunk in the hallway, and the next moment we beheld Louise's sturdy frame in the doorway, sheathed in a faux leopard robe and shod in her perennial Dr. Scholl's. We greeted her like a lost relation. She gave us one of her tough-woman grins—mouth truculent, eyes twinkling and coy. I didn't think she remembered us, but she played like a savvy detective off our familiarity with her.

Riding the crest of one of her good moods, she lifted a cut-glass bowl from Mom's dresser, turned it round and round like a priestess with a chalice. "Quite a beauty," she said. "Worth at least $1500. So often they don't realize," she went on, "when they have something of value. I have a nose for it myself. It was part of my training and I always said you get what you pay for. Is this your mother? I assumed that. I wouldn't recommend leaving your mother's bowl lying out in a place like this. It isn't exactly church. But you know, it might as well be."

Then the wave broke, her authority with it. She asked plaintively, "You wouldn't happen to know how a person gets outside?"

Upstairs Spruce extended onto a broad terrace, built on Pine's roof, where Louise used to sit in the sun for hours. All her pacing the halls, her obsessive games of solitaire were just ways to mark time until she could get outside.

We guessed that it had been her appetite for fresh air that got her demoted to Pine, where there is none.

For Louise could still dress and groom herself, she was continent, she was articulate and coherent, though her original premises might have derived from a world of her own.

She could deal several different solitaires, and in my casual observation, didn't cheat at them. But she was a wrench in the system. She had strong feelings, desires, moods.

When Louise was down, she criticized and complained, she refused to eat, she pined for escape, even begged for death. Fortunately—she might have said unfortunately—she didn't wield a cane. But we suspected she had tried to bolt. In Spruce instead of a locked door, the number-pad guarded the elevator. Easy enough to wait for it to arrive on Spruce's floor, then slip into the empty car before the door rolled shut. And go for a long walk outside.

What did you do with a Louise once you caught her? We guessed you moved her down to Pine, put in an alarm that would be activated by the bracelet you buckled on her wrist—a system you tried to finance by charging a monthly fee to buckle a similar bracelet onto every other semi-mobile body in sight.

⁓

It was late autumn, almost a year after Dad's death. Cathy and arrived for a Saturday morning visit and proposed an *expeditio* to Duke Gardens to see if the chrysanthemums were still in flower.

There was still no sign of the garden promised the ambulatory residents of Pine by the administration upstairs, who like the residents of Pine, seemed to have lost their sense of time. And like the residents of Pine, their original premises derived from a world of their own.

For them the residents downstairs were dolls in an elaborate game of house. Dolls didn't crave fresh air, like Louise. Dolls didn't keep on aging. The ambulatory ones didn't soon take to wheelchairs and finally die waiting for a grandiose idea to produce one real sprout.

Actually Mother wasn't waiting. There was too much going on outside her window for her to lament what wasn't. On some days children assembled in the late afternoons for ballet lessons. On others, bad children tried to peek in at her and catch her in her nightgown.

In fact there was so much going on in Pine from her point of view that she would probably rather not have ventured out to Duke Gardens with us. It was a lot of trouble for her to move her body, and she seemed happy curled into one of the wing chairs beside the central nurses' station taking in the buzz of gossip and shoptalk.

Sometimes Chris found her sitting behind the station *helping* the receptionist. Usually Louise was back there too, having been invited to clear some space on the desk and lay out her cards.

But Cathy and I still assumed that it was better to *do something* than not do *anything*. And Mother didn't want to disappoint us. We bundled her up against the wind and signed her out.

Proudly we punched in the three numbers for escape—there was nothing wrong with *our* memories—and proceeded through the door. Immediately an alarm began its deafening clang.

Mother slumped forward as if a heavy rain were beating on her back. The charge nurse came running with a key to make the noise stop. She pointed to the plastic bracelet on Mother's wrist. "Sorry," we said. "We didn't notice that she had one of those things on."

"Don't worry about it," the nurse said. "We keep forgetting to remind the family. It's so crazy." She looked taxed.

Among the old people planted in various corners around us, even the most glazed looked electrified by the noise.

"You mean these bracelets haven't cut down on the large number of residents escaping from Pine?" Cathy asked.

The nurse grimaced. "Can you believe it?"

రాం

There were times when it happened quickly, easily—if we didn't talk about it, didn't give her a chance to remember that her body had forgotten. Just expect her to do it, we thought, and some days our mother was able to fold herself into the front seat of a car.

This would not be such a day. She bent slightly at the knees and hips then froze. I finally had to topple her while Cathy caught and tried to arrange her, urging her to lean her head against the back of the seat and lower her feet from midair onto the floor. Mother chattered nonsense all the while, as if to distract us from the embarrassment.

Once underway she commented politely on the scenery—"A lot of the houses around here have their gardens right in their garden."

Which was more than anyone could say about the fantasy garden at Evergreen.

In the parking lot we faced what we certainly deserved, the physics of getting her out of the car. There was no just doing it. The casual order didn't work, the extended hands, coaxing words.

Then it dawned on both of us: the last thing *she* deserved was to feel that she had failed when it was *our* failure that had dragged her out here. *Our* deafness to emotional tones.

"You know, I think it's just too chilly out for me," I said, and climbed back in the car. Cathy agreed, then drove right past the Italian restaurant we'd talked about trying again. We'd taken Mother there the month before, maneuvering her into the chair, heaving the chair up to the table, and then constantly coaching her—*maybe if you poked at it with your fork; no, don't pick up the pasta.* Last time she'd delicately spooned at the vegetables printed on the tablecloth. People had stared.

"What about good old McDonald's?" Cathy threw out when she saw it ahead.

"Your father loved him," Mother said.

And so we stopped for what would be her last supper outside of Pine. After all, fast food involved no decorum. With me gripping Mother's wrists and Cathy sprawled across the gear shift pushing up from behind, we passed the point of paralyzed equilibrium, and we were able to launch her from the seat. We each took an arm, and she shuffled forward on the balls of her feet.

Inside she raved about the décor. We sat by a sunny window, beyond which two real children really were playing on a red and yellow tubular slide. "They like the outdoors," Mother observed. "They feel there's an island of beauty out there."

She could no longer pull the milkshake up through the straw so we fed it to her with a spoon.

⁓

Cathy and I spent the nights of our visits at Chris's house now, talking late, sharing our sense of doom. Chris, citing genetics, feared that we were witnessing what lay ahead for each of us.

Cathy, resolutely absent-minded and cynical, asked, "What do you mean, *ahead*?"

Hoisting the fallen flag of optimism, I questioned whether our mother even had Alzheimer's. "Look at Betty, look at Lorraine. She doesn't act at all like them."

"She has something," Cathy said.

Well, but think nurture over nature, I suggested. Think of the number of major surgeries Dad's body had endured, the number of general anesthetics. Think of all Mother's antidepressants and, my god, the shock treatments. That stuff had to have taken a big toll on their brains.

Chris repeated what the head of the memory clinic at Duke Hospital had told him: there were no studies that correlated any of *that stuff* with organic brain disease.

"Did you ever ask," I wondered, "whether any studies about that stuff have actually been done?"

Worrying about our later selves was a luxury compared to worrying about our mother now. An eternity ago when we still whispered the *A* word, we imagined the horror of her empty breathing body, blank eyes in a blank face, the spirit fled. But after a year of visiting Pine, we realized there were as many faces of Alzheimer's or dementia—*something*—as there were residents, and none blank.

Each was a scrim for the spirit locked in every cell, for which there was no clean escape.

Our fears shifted. What if her swallow reflex shut down while she was still the unmistakable person she was? What if she still knew us, still talked to us, shared intriguing things with us like, "There's a misery flare that's usable right in the middle of the floor," yet was no longer able to eat? Did we inflict the feeding tube? How would we prepare her to starve?

While we worried about the end, once more the middle uncorked an ambush.

On our next visit Mother wasn't in her room. In fact, her room wasn't in her room, but in the one across the hall where our father had died. Betty had been moved also, and where the two rooms used to be stood a sheetrock barrier that narrowed the hallway to a dark passage and didn't muffle the noises of demolition and remodeling or the smell of plaster dust and paint.

Now that all the rooms on that one corridor were occupied, by a population whom sudden change could *agitate*, the administration upstairs had decided to make a massive change, with a complete remodel.

The garden would be just part of it. There were also plans for a special lounge and dining area and for a wall to seal off a whole Alzheimer's wing from the rest of Pine, with another locked door.

A nurse explained that the executive director didn't like the non-bedridden residents sitting behind the central desk with the staff, or lined up so visibly in the wing chairs nearby, "like birds on a wire." She didn't want them spoiling the effect when she brought visitors through to show off her geriatric utopia. After all, the executive director had once boasted that Pine would never smell of urine while she was in charge.

Half-heartedly we objected to the whole project, but we could have predicted the words we would hear in response. Evergreen was creating a model Alzheimer's unit, cutting-edge, state-of-the art. Everyone was very excited about it.

Betty wasn't excited about it, we said. For the two days of our visit, the displaced Betty's eyebrows were knit in a fierce frown. She made her way cautiously along the tightened hallway, scolding the world and snarling if you smiled at her.

"Well, it's a free market," came the reply. "You can always move your mother somewhere else."

This new mother of ours was much more flexible than we were. It was almost a joke on us. All those years of pleading with her to look at the good side, assume the best, and now she was finally living our advice.

The mess of construction in the middle of her world didn't bother her. From her garbled comments, we gathered that she was having the kitchen remodeled, and such things took time if you wanted to do them right. "This place is a good place with these kids here," she assured us. "Have you ever heard of people being turned away?"

Not turned away, no. But treated as pawns in a game? Mice in an experiment? Shabby furniture you have to hide? What about mindless, heartless creatures that might have to be dropped in their tracks?

We had convinced ourselves the latter danger was past. Mother was going to be all right in Pine because the everyday staff was kind and sensitive, and besides, she'd gotten to be so nice, she wasn't going to do something like swing a cane around and scare people.

We were wrong. The same delusions that buffered her against sorrow, frustration, and fear would make her a target.

A brand new Fellow from Duke had been turned loose among the residents. Eager to practice medicine, he discovered that our mother "experienced hallucinations" and that she often woke up in the middle of the night. He decided that both of these habits posed serious problems and had to be addressed. His solution was to prescribe daily doses of Haldol.

Although Chris thought he had an agreement with the staff doctor that he, Chris, would be informed if any of our mother's medications were changed, he was never told that Haldol had been added to her regimen. Instead he watched in bewilderment as her spirits began to droop. She was crying again during his visits. She fell out of bed; she fell being helped from a chair. Within three weeks, her right hand had contracted to the point that her fingernails gouged her palm.

Finally Chris thought to ask about her drugs and learned the incredible truth. Of course he insisted the doses be stopped, of course we wrote an angry letter, of course we were answered with the suggestion that maybe our mother would be happier somewhere else. The people upstairs didn't get it.

As far as they were concerned, neither did we. The staff doctor with the soulful eyes wrote back, deeply wounded. How could we think, he asked, that a physician would agree to consult with family members over a patient's medications? How could we not see that such a practice would significantly interfere with the physician's ability to deliver to that patient the optimum care?

⮞ 9 ⮜

LOCKED IN THE PAST

Housekeeping had worked overtime cleaning and deodoriz-
ing, and the nursing assistants had started at dawn, bathing,
shampooing, and dolling up the aged bodies for the afternoon reception. The unveiling. Reporters from the *Herald*
were invited, along with doctors from Duke and numerous
pillars of the Durham community. There was a spread of little sandwiches and cookies and a bowl of punch.

As far as the administration was concerned, the Evergreen
Alzheimer's Wing and Wandering Garden was the jewel in
its crown, its ticket into the Nursing Home Hall of Fame.

So much depended upon your point of view. What we
saw when we arrived the next weekend was a wall where our
mother used to sit in her wing chair—a wall, a locked door
and a little sign that said, *To enter push button marked EXIT.*

We obeyed. The door opened. But before we could step

inside, Louise had hurled herself into our arms.

"Why won't they help me die," she wailed, trying to wrench free as we eased her back where she now belonged. "It's the only thing I want. I can't live like this."

The door clicked shut behind us. Its inside surface was meticulously painted to look like floor-to-ceiling bookshelves. Louise glared wildly from them to us. She couldn't process what she saw, and for once had nothing to say to cover her puzzled helplessness.

"It must be terrible for you," Cathy said.

Louise stopped struggling. Her expression smoothed to serene. "Thank you," she said. "I'm glad someone will say that." Then she added, "I'm so healthy I'm never going to die. I'll be stuck here forever."

For reasons known only to the director of Pine, the one with the graduate training in Fine Arts, *here* had been transformed into a decorator's version of The Fifties.

The space that once belonged to Betty and Mom now displayed a sofa covered in a splashy purple, red, and turquoise print and three chairs: purple plush Danish modern, aqua leather, and a turquoise canvas sling, one of those butterfly designs that not even the able-bodied can get in and out of. A kidney-shaped coffee table held vintage magazines, *The Saturday Evening Post, Colliers*, and *Look*.

In the far corner stood the exhibit "kitchen," complete with the empty shell of a range, Melmac dishes, and two dinette sets of shiny red Formica, red vinyl, and chrome.

Cathy and I couldn't process what we were seeing.

On the purple wall behind the sofa, an Edward Hopper print exuded gloom. The other white walls were festooned with 78 rpm records. At one end of the room stood a life-sized cardboard cutout of James Dean in jeans, a T-shirt, with a cigarette hanging from the corner of his mouth. Vamping him from another corner, in a red, strapless gown, was a cardboard Marilyn Monroe.

Our eyes must have been asking, *is this for real?* Patrice, one of the nursing assistants who had volunteered to work all her shifts in the new unit, wasn't sure either. She grinned gamely as she settled Louise at one of the kitchen tables with a deck of cards. "They did a good job on the garden," she said. "But this just has folks wondering."

"Why in the world The Fifties?" I asked the LPN who seemed almost my age. She was feeding Mother her meds crushed into chocolate pudding. The bravado days were over, when she could pop them into her own mouth all at once. She couldn't always swallow at will anymore, and since the Haldol experiment, both hands had curled into claws.

"An age of innocence?" Cathy suggested.

"Let's see, you would have been in your thirties back then," I told Mother. "Maybe they think that was your prime?"

"I certainly had a household full of twins and ice cream," Mother said.

The LPN shook her head. "If I ever land in a nursing home, it better not remind me of bell bottoms and Pink Floyd. That was a real bad time in my life."

"Do you suppose they'll redecorate for The Sixties in ten years?" Cathy wondered.

A dapper man in V-neck and plaid shirt had been listening from the sofa, a newcomer, who now observed, "They have that funny hour system, and if you don't get a lot of it, you don't get any."

I knew just what he meant.

༄

The Wandering Garden was lovely. Bounded on three sides by the stucco walls of the building, its fourth side was a steep hill planted with trees and shrubs, sloping to a stone fountain at its base.

A concrete path looped off a terrace lined with flower beds of impatiens, petunias, and marigolds. There were wooden benches, two umbrella tables with chairs, and a wooden gate that served no purpose besides the challenge of opening and closing it once you'd passed through.

Most impressive of all, on our next month's visit, we found a young man scrambling up and down a long ladder in order to paint a mural, three stories high, on the far blank wall. Over the weekend the rustic scene took shape, meadow and stream on the right, trees on the left, and purple mountains in the background, framed by a blue sky of challah-plump clouds. Its accurate perspective brought the illusion of unending space.

All this state-of-the-art, separate Alzheimer's unit needed were state-of-the-art Alzheimer's patients: benign bodies which had lost most of their abilities but could still walk, minds vacant of significant and potentially disruptive feelings, yet which still could appreciate natural beauty. Such human oxymorons were hard to come by.

Mary Beach had Alzheimer's but spent her waking hours now in a wheelchair. Same with Serena with the rippling platinum hair. Professor Mandelbaum had died long before the wing was ready.

Betty's family had transferred her to the Methodist home. Rumor had it that they had run out of money, but she'd never laughed again after the remodeling evicted her from her room.

Lorraine's husband P. J. moved her to one of the other corridors in Pine. He thought the locked unit was an accident waiting to happen: ten fragile, unpredictable individuals in the charge of one nursing assistant; an infinite menu of possible emergencies. How could one person handle both a crisis and a race to the door to key in the *open sesame* and summon help?

We considered moving our mother. In the arms of Patrice or Barbara, the other nursing assistant who had volunteered for the unit, she was barely able to tiptoe the few steps from her bed to the purple plush chair that became her favorite. Long gone was her ability to wander on her own in the garden beyond the windows and glass door.

But it turned out she was quite proud of the jazzed-up digs, which she assumed were hers. "I think it's a nice thing and a pleasure to have it," she told us.

A new resident, Dorothy, formerly the physician in charge of Duke's student health services, was ambulatory at first, but a garden and bright colors couldn't penetrate her constant, inconsolable sadness, alleviated only by spells of scrubbing the backs of her hands with her own spit. She took a couple of falls and within a month joined the chair-bound.

Another new resident, the former mayor of Durham, could walk with help, but we would never see him step out for a stroll. The disease seemed to have left him relentlessly irritated, and though he had lost language entirely, he spent his public time making grunting noises of complaint. When food could be cajoled into his mouth, he chewed but then returned it to his plate. Soon he would stop coming out of his room at all, and then one weekend we would find it empty.

Emma kept her room at the end of the Alzheimer's corridor, but we didn't believe she even had Alzheimer's. We suspected she had always just been ornery and now she was very old. She chugged along in her self-styled outfits, using all her concentration to push her walker.

On the other side of the locked door there were women just like Emma pushing their walkers down the other corridors. In fact a few months after its unveiling, there was no difference between the population inside the Alzheimer's Wing and the population on the other corridors of Pine. On each side of the door, some could walk, and some never got out of bed, and some spent their waking hours in wheelchairs.

Inside the unit, aged bodies were made to conform to garish Danish modern furniture. Outside, aged bodies gradually reappeared in the wing chairs around the nurses' station, lined up again like "birds on a wire."

There were two exceptions. Locked back in The Fifties, under the sexy gazes of Marilyn Monroe and James Dean, Louise and the new man, Ray, paced and hyperventilated like caged animals. Because orders from the administration decreed that the camouflaged door must remain shut.

At that moment in their shrinking lives, Louise and Ray came closest to fitting the profile of the Alzheimer's Patient which the wing had been built for—if it had been built for the residents at all. They could walk, and though they may not have been interested in the autumn foliage and flowers, they craved fresh air on their faces, in their lungs. They wanted to go and go, they wanted to get somewhere.

The garden was a tease. Louise asked permission to go outside, but once through the door, she walked the loop, opened and shut the gate, and that was it. Maybe it had been better, more cathartic, marching up and down, up and down, the crossed hallways of Pine's main area. Now she caught sight of them through an occasional opening in the wall—a glimpse of her old beaten track stretching away from the nurses' station, beckoning. At least she thought it was an opening. Before she could get across the room to slip through, it was gone, and in its place the floor-to-ceiling books.

"My life is joke," she moaned. "The whole world would be better off if I were dead."

"You shouldn't talk like that," Patrice would answer. "I wouldn't be better off."

"Of course you wouldn't. You've got a job."

"You can't die until your teach me all those card games."

"Just say the word. I could start yesterday."

"Well, I was wondering if you might like to get in a little walk first?"

Louise seemed touched, humbled, by Patrice's thoughtfulness. "Would you mind?" she asked softly.

"No, I don't mind at all."

Louise hadn't removed her sweater since her last trip around the loop, ten minutes ago. She trudged outside and made the circuit once more.

We had settled Mother in the purple chair and pulled its purple hassock around close enough that I could caress and comfort her—we had just worked a lamb's wool-and-plastic brace onto one of her hands, still contracted thanks to the past barrage of Haldol, and unclenching her fingers had caused her pain.

"How are you doing?" I asked her now, still feeling the bite of guilt.

"I'll be back in a little while," she assured me.

Cathy was on the couch with Ray beside her. Dorothy was part of the circle in her reclining wheel-chair, taking after Mary Beach in her determination to remove her socks. Her whimpering filled the background as soft-spoken Ray told us about his life.

We had already heard from the nurses that he'd been one of the first people to occupy an apartment upstairs and that he'd served as the head of the residents' association. Then he'd lost his wife to cancer last year, watching and worrying by her bedside for weeks. Now he was remembering his childhood, growing up in a cabin on the Kansas prairie, eleven to a room, rattling off names and family relationships we couldn't keep straight. He worked his way around to Duke's business school, its continuing education program for executives, which he had helped found.

We let him know we were very impressed.

He gathered imaginary papers from the coffee table, then pinched up a piece of lint from the carpet and wiped it onto the table. "All set?" he asked, popping to his feet and surveying the room. "Did I throw my cap over in this direction?"

We pointed it out on the table. He bent over and grabbed at the wheel of Dorothy's chair instead. He rose empty-handed, then sat back down on the couch.

"Were you thinking of going for a walk in the garden?" I asked.

"I believe I was," he said.

Cathy stood and gazed out the window. "Isn't the new mural something?" she said. "I just noticed the little stream there, winding through that field."

Ray was on his feet again. "It connects to a pretty good-sized lake a few miles down the road," he said, then managed to grab his cap and was out the door.

Cathy and I asked each other questions about our children, husbands, gardens, reenacting conversations we'd already had on the trip down, for our mother's entertainment. She listened contentedly, contributing a random comment when the spirit moved her. Maybe Dorothy was capable of curiosity, or maybe the sound of our voices simply soothed her, because her whimpering quieted.

"Uh oh," Cathy said, suddenly standing. From her seat on the couch, she'd spotted Ray clambering up the steep hill dodging, the new trees and shrubs. Soon he reached the chain link fence at the top and started inching his way along it, hand over hand. Maybe he was looking for a way to get to that lake; maybe he was just trying not to slide down this very real slippery slope into the fountain.

He was a small, tidy man, his hair slicked back with oil, his top shirt-button buttoned, his slacks buckled high over the slightest paunch, but he forged ahead with such resolve he seemed the incarnation of something primal, heroic—the desire to live free.

Cathy and I had to ask each other if we should go after him. We were stalling. We so wanted him somehow, magically, to escape.

Patrice came back into the room.

"Ray's probably not where he should be out there," Cathy said, a little shamefaced. "I was just going to go get him."

Patrice bolted out the door and up the hill. When they both returned, she was huffing and puffing and shaking her head. Ray breathed smoothly but concentration creased his brow—*next time*, he seemed to be thinking. *Maybe next time.*

⁜

Mother's naps consumed more and more of the time between meals. So Cathy and I sat in her darkened room while she dozed, and performed our discussions there. It was actually easier now to visit, oddly restful, now that we'd been forced to give up on *expeditios*. There was nothing to do but put our arms around her stooped shoulders, stroke her twisted hands, and listen to the fits and starts of sentences, tuning to the rhythm of meaning underneath the ruined melody.

And there were pleasant surprises. A rap-rap on Mother's half-closed door one afternoon and Marie's dazzling white head appeared, her uncertain smile. "Come on in and have a lollipop," she said.

She was a little heavier than when we'd last seen her up in Spruce. Her once lovely lavender sweater was rumpled and linty, and its buttons were not in their correct buttonholes. But she was an old friend. Without prompting, she shuffled over to the side of Mother's bed, patted her knot of a hand and called her Evelyn. We were positive she remembered us too, that her delight and the ferocity of her hugs were more than a reflection of our own. As if to clinch this, she tugged at the toe of one of Mother's stockinged feet and said, "I thought I'd seen them somewhere before."

Mother looked smug, as though taking credit for Marie's arrival. "Where's Shirley?" she asked her.

Who's Shirley? Cathy mouthed to me.

"Don't tell me she's hiding," Mother said, sort of haughtily, stiff-lipped.

"How come you're trying to talk without moving your mouth?" I asked her.

She started to giggle then suppressed it. "I don't want to break my neck."

"I don't know where Aunt Ruth has gone," Marie said.

"Was she one of your favorites?" Cathy asked.

"Who?" Marie asked back.

"Your Aunt Ruth."

"It's hard to find people who know each other," Marie said. "Well, I'm glad to see Evelyn with all that good stuff around her."

Cathy and I assumed she was referring to us and beamed. Then she patted Mother's feet again and told us she had to be going. We exchanged more hugs and she shuffled out. All at once I wanted to cry. It wasn't grief but gratitude. Marie was where Mother had been a year ago. Mother was so much less than that now, and yet still *here*, an undeniable soul.

Then Marie was back. She peeked in the door as if she'd never peeked in before.

"Come on in, Marie," Cathy called out heartily.

"Well, I don't know," she said.

"How have you been?" I asked.

"Something very exciting happened," Marie said, "but I can't remember what it was."

"You've moved," Cathy suggested. "You have a new room now. Do you like it?"

"If we can come together after we separate and realize we're all part of the same package," Marie said.

"It's just great to see a familiar face," I told her. "Isn't it, Mom?"

"She's that girl we think of as a semi-colon," Mother said.

"She's a good friend," Cathy said. "You two have known each other for a couple of years now."

"We had half a dozen days when we were all lying on top of each other," said Marie.

❧

Our mother's body grew more rigid. Despite experimental doses of Synemet, the Parkinson's medication they'd refused our father, she couldn't flex or unflex any muscles at will. When we first laid her down, she couldn't rest her head on the pillow or stretch her legs along the mattress. Her body stayed locked in the angles it had assumed while slumped in a chair.

We hated having to ask Patrice or Barbara to change her Depends or get her into her nightgown, but we couldn't perform these jobs ourselves anymore without our clumsiness inflicting pain. Those two women managed them quickly and gently. Resilient, resourceful, and inexhaustibly kind, they belong in their own Hall of Fame.

They had learned to maneuver bodies into, out of, and around a labyrinth of crazy furniture, all form and no function. Single-handedly they each synchronized the daily functions of all the patients in their charge, wove randomness and unreason into a comfortable, sturdy nest.

Barbara brought brisk, witty efficiency to her job. Patrice added an aesthetic dimension, vases of flowers and baskets of fruit, moussed hair-dos for her charges, and rouged cheeks.

Together they had turned a bizarre, almost perverse idea into a clean, well-lighted, nurturing place.

We helped Mother out to the living room after a nap, lowered her into her plush chair, and on the sofa, Ray woke with a start. "I apologize for not standing up when you came in the room," he said.

"That's OK," I told him. "You were dozing."

"Then I apologize for dozing," he said.

"You have every right to doze," I said.

He looked pleased. "I've had a long day."

On the kitchen counter sat a novelty tape player designed to look like one of those jukebox selectors in fifties diners. Cathy went over and picked one of the three authorized tapes, Johnny Mathis, The Platters, or early rock and roll.

Mother asked her what she was doing, and she called back, "Putting on some music."

"My gosh, what a job," Mother said, as Mathis's crooning filled the room. "Are you happy, Cathy honey?"

Cathy answered that she was.

"I am too," Mother said.

When the line came, Cathy sang along with it: "Until the twelfth of never, I'll still be loving you."

"I'll love you till the day I die," Mother said.

Marie's husband had been an orchestra conductor. Now as she sat at one of the tables listening to the tape, I realized that her fingernails on the Formica were clicking a piano accompaniment. Where Johnny Mathis's tenor rose, her right hand stretched away from her left. As far as I could tell, she was hitting every note. I asked her if she used to play the piano.

"Oh, a little bit," she said.

"I bet you're being modest," I said. The fingers kept dancing a life of their own. "You were pretty good, weren't you?"

Marie didn't answer. She truly wasn't sure.

Louise flounced in wearing a slinky nightgown and negligee. Ray, still socially aware, made a nervous, giggling noise.

"I suppose I should get dressed," Louise said. "But I spent so many years getting dressed.' She looked right at Ray. "Dressed to the teeth."

"People will think you're selling them," Marie said, her hands halting in mid-tune. She'd had her eye on Ray too.

"I don't suppose I can interest anyone in a walk," Louise asked, still looking at Ray.

Ray seemed flustered. You could tell he'd been taught never to disappoint a lady. "I don't think just now," he said.

"I've got to get out of this kitchen," Louise said.

Marie had shuffled over to face the cutout of James Dean. Now she struck a pose that mirrored his, hand on hip, hip canted seductively. "Is this gentleman," she began to ask, then paused. "What's his official capacity?"

"That's James Dean," I told her. "A movie star who was killed in a car accident before his time."

"I knew him from somewhere around," Marie said.

"He isn't real," I said, wondering what I meant.

Cathy pulls the figure away from the wall, turned it sideways. "See," she said, "cardboard."

Blank looks all around.

When she set him back against the wall, Marie leaned towards him and whispered, "Do you remember me?"

Cathy dragged Marilyn Monroe to the middle of the room. "OK, who knows who this is?"

"Lucille Ball," Mom said.

"Marilyn Lyn," said Ray.

Louise nodded. "She had a rough go of it, a pathetic life. She had a good education too. We were very close friends."

"There's still a mystery here," said Marie.

⌁ 10 ⌁

ENTROPY

Things fall apart, old orders collapse.

Life wears away at the rules.

An abandoned elementary school was gutted by flames, and the executive director's teenage son was arrested and charged with arson. She and her family decided to move out of state. The administration upstairs fell into more disarray.

Downstairs in Pine someone took the liberty to suggest that maybe it wouldn't be such a bad idea to leave the door to the Alzheimer's wing open sometimes. People kept forgetting to close it anyway, inviting disaster, yet none had occurred.

Very well, came the decree from above. As long as it was for one hour only and always at the same time of day.

Soon from one to two o'clock in the afternoon, Louise and Ray had permission to walk somewhere else besides the single loop of the garden, and they began to do so with great energy and purpose, marching back and forth over the threshold as the minutes ticked away. They could never quite get enough. When the time was up and the bookcase mysteriously reappeared, they were brought up short in their tracks. They looked around baffled, betrayed.

Then the official hour started to stretch. Nursing assistants from Pine's main area began taking their breaks around the kitchen tables, preferring the bright, eccentric décor and garden views to their sterile canteen. They popped in their own Nineties tapes, Motown and R & B. Someone went out to Burger King, then chomping on hamburgers and French fries, they told stories about husbands, boyfriends, kids, whooping with disbelief and laughter.

Someone's adolescent son shambled in, wide jeans stacked around his ankles in elephantine folds, a cool bounce to his step. He wanted to borrow the keys to his mother's car. "No way," she said. But he had to pick up something for school. "What happened to the legs god give you?" she said. He shambled out.

If Mother was awake, she took it all in from her purple chair, her lips pursed in the mischievous smile of someone getting away with something.

Finally, although the sign on the wall beside the bookcase still warned, *This door must be closed at all times*, the only time it actually was closed was during meals. The flow of activity in Pine almost returned to its former freedom. Other nursing assistants dropped in to chat with Patrice or Barbara. And as the quickest route to the Garden, The Fifties museum hosted a steady parade of residents from upstairs accompanied by visiting family and friends.

Come spring, Lorraine Burns's husband P. J. brought down his tape player and held sing-alongs out by the fountain, waving his arms to coax a word or a phrase from his audience, which watched him curiously from a semi-circle of wheelchairs. When he snapped in a tape or "Old Mill Stream," he rendered the lyrics extra carefully, directing certain lines to his silent, blinking wife.

⌘

Our mother's chemistry was breaking down. She was losing the balance that held her poised above the turbulence of pain. As winter deepened, she began to suffer quiet, but more and more protracted seizures.

Chris was terribly upset by the deterioration, and also by a conversation with the staff doctor. It reminded him too much of the interchanges he'd had with the man before our father crashed. "Same time of year, same tone, same what if's. It's like he's trying to prepare me for the end because *he's* decided it's time for it to happen."

The doctor was choosing now to let us know the discouraging results of a swallowing test on our mother, which he'd apparently had on file for several months. The doctor was also wondering whether we wanted to invoke "extraordinary measures" to keep her alive, claiming that we'd never clarified our wishes on that score.

Chris thought he had made our wishes clear to the doctor

on many earlier occasions: no extraordinary measures, just comfort care.

Cathy and I witnessed a seizure firsthand when we visited in February. She was dozing in the purple chair, and as I leaned over to kiss her forehead, she opened her eyes and without a second's hesitation asked, "When I go down that lonely road, will you be waiting for me at the end?"

"No," I told her, "But Dad will. He's there watching for you. He'll help you along."

That seemed to satisfy her. Cathy and I pulled up a chair and the hassock and settled in to enjoy her presence. I felt somehow full and complete in that arrangement, as if we were two children, sitting at our mother's knee. As though we were finally, effortlessly receiving the blessing which we'd struggled all our lives to deserve.

She volunteered a string of unrelated half-thoughts and strange words—*what's good for us when we're unpayetic, just rising out of the chavis damp.* At first we listened and nodded, as if we understood, but that made her try even harder. She seemed almost desperate to keep us entertained. One burden Alzheimer's often spares its victims—the pressure of self-conscious social awareness—would oppress her to the end.

I took advantage of a pause to ask how her breakfast was.

"I made some rice pudding," she said. "Put cream on it and it was filling."

"Sounds delicious."

"That's what Billy said. You don't know that he's come to land. He'd like to go to China. He's a frightened person."

Billy again, I was thinking—someone else, an absence, a ghost she would clutch until the end. The old resentment flared. Cathy and I had set everything aside to spend a weekend with her; we didn't need to be regaled with stories of seeing Billy, receiving presents from Billy, of being made so happy by Billy?

Today the old jealousy quickly shifted into alarm. Her body had started to tremble everywhere, her muscles so tense that I feared they would snap. From her lips drawn back in a grimace came the full-throated sounds of grief.

Terrified we jumped to our feet, stroked her face, arms, called her name. As if from an enormous distance she made an answering sound.

"Are you in pain?" Cathy asked.

"Yes," came the response from far away.

"Where, Mom?"

"In the parking lot," she gasped.

"Could we help you lie down?"

Her fists clenched tighter, her nails digging into her palms. She struggled to force a reply: "I'd rather just sit here and moan."

I went to look for Barbara. When we returned, the translucent skin of Mom's face was slick with sweat. Barbara shook her head sadly. "Afterwards she's so sopping wet," she said, "I've got to change all her clothes."

The three of us murmured reassurance, but there was nothing else to do but watch until the seizure subsided. "She suffers so much," Barbara muttered under her breath, her own face pinched with pain. Her guard was down. Unlike the doctors, for Barbara the appearance of anguish *was* anguish, as real as her own.

A stunning, self-possessed young woman whose cropped hair accentuated high cheekbones and caramel skin, Barbara had captivated our mother from first meeting. Mother decided she was Egyptian, and whenever Barbara came into view and offered a gruff greeting or question, Mother would go speechless. A look would come over her, exalted, embarrassed, expectant, that reminded me of my own days of youthful crushes.

Once when Barbara left the room, we remarked to Mother, "You sure seemed glad to see her."

"But I don't dare say so," Mother replied. "Someone might come and take her away."

We realized that the affection was mutual. Though her style with us was clipped, no-nonsense, impersonal, she and our mother shared a relationship we'd never know about. Maybe Mother had managed to offer her deserved praise, or maybe doses of well-intended aphorism: "you've got to beat your drum"; "there are winter things and summer things, all in a pattern." And maybe Barbara had been able to listen through the "crazy language" and hear concern.

The next time a seizure occurred that weekend, we were helping Mother stretch out on her bed. I remembered how our chatting voices had soothed her to sleep in the past, but neither Cathy nor I could get a conversation going under the circumstances. In desperation, I darted out to the living

room and came back with the old *Saturday Evening Post* from
the coffee table. I began to read the short-short story aloud,
which turned out to portray a mother teaching her sixth-
grade son a lesson about money.

Detritus of an innocent age indeed, the story was sim-
plistic, the dialogue stilted, but maybe Billy's ghost cast an
intriguing shadow across its single page. Or maybe the seizure was already letting go by the time I'd launched into the
opening paragraph. Her body did grow still. She did seem to
be listening.

The following day at the first sign of trembling, sweat
beading on the upper lip, I ran for the magazine and started
to read the ridiculous story again, my voice getting louder
and louder as the boy chose to squander a nickel on ice cream
instead of putting it in his bank. It worked much more slowly
this time to break the seizure. If it worked at all.

Cathy and I carried home the painful image of her distress. The end must be approaching, we told each other.
She couldn't go on this way. Her difficulty with swallowing loomed large. No matter how benignly the staff doctor
described death by starvation, something had got to happen
to rescue us from the horror of having to authorize that fate
for her.

Then Chris called. The staff doctor had suggested dis-
continuing her small dose of Zoloft. Chris agreed. There
was nothing to lose. And for several days now, she had been
seizure-free. Hardly a *new lease on life*, but we'd settle for the
reprieve. And the staff doctor *had* checked with Chris first

before doing anything. That in itself seemed sufficient reason for elation.

The next months brought other changes. During one visit, Emma all at once vomited onto her dinner tray. While we scrambled around toweling up the mess, Patrice helped her back to her room and tucked her into bed. Stomach virus, we assumed, rolling our eyes at the prospect of its spreading through the unit. The next morning Emma was dead.

We took to walking the corridor when we first arrived for our visit to make sure everyone was still alive. One month we found Ray's room empty and his name removed from the door. We couldn't believe it. Not Ray, not the most *normal* of the wing's residents, the least advanced in his disease. The gentleman who never complained, who ate his meals quietly, with perfect manners, while next to him Louise cursed the food, lashed out at the whole world, and begged to die.

Then Barbara told us the good news. The impossible had occurred: gravity had been reversed. Ray was back upstairs in Spruce. He had been put on an experimental drug for Alzheimer's and it was working. Later the charge nurse would elaborate. It wasn't a cure, but it would buy him a little time, slow the progress of the disease. We wondered how much self-awareness it would buy. Would he remember the vortex he'd been pulled from? Would he treasure each rescued day, understanding that the downspin must win in the end?

A TV hour had been added to the schedule of the wing. A large screen was wheeled out to the center of the living room, the residents were assembled on the sofa and chairs around it, and a video anthology of *I Love Lucy* episodes was slipped into the VCR.

Until it was displaced by *Eastenders* in the eighties, *Lucy* was Mother's favorite show. She who never got jokes would laugh so hard at Lucy's antics that she'd have to run to the bathroom. Desi Arnaz and his Latin accent must have reminded her of her own autocratic Spanish father, the man who'd squelched her mother, against whom she herself had had to fight for every inch of psychic space. Each time Lucy bested Desi, maybe it sparked an explosion of delight and relief.

Now Lucy chattered on against a counterpoint of canned laughter. Behind the TV at one of the tables, Louise played an impassive game of solitaire, while in front of it, Mom, Marie, and a new man, whose brain had been injured in an accident, stared into space.

Our mother could no longer be stood on her feet at all and had inherited someone's wheelchair. Chris had thought to have her bridges removed, which improved her oral hygiene considerably but left her with just her twelve front teeth. Her mouth hung open most of the time. The words she strung together lent themselves less and less to interpretation, as syntax collapsed.

She'd grown thinner. She was now one of the women for whom the kitchen sent down a plate of pale, homogenized mounds. We tried to discourage her hands from jerking their way into the purees while encouraging her mouth to open for them. Patrice prided herself on being able to get her to eat by coating the front of each spoonful of meat or vegetable mush with chocolate ice cream.

More and more the clenching of her teeth seemed willful. I was sure her eyes asked us not to force any more. I think she knew she was having trouble swallowing, and I knew she'd been afraid for many years of choking to death. She'd told a story more than once of eating steak at an Officers' Club and having a piece of it stick in her throat. She'd had to run to the ladies' room and gag herself in order to dislodge it, succeeding right before she was going to pass out.

There'd also been a choking incident in the dining room up in Spruce, during which one of the staff had performed the Heimlich maneuver on her. A wisp of *leit motif*, those close calls had often woven themselves into her "crazy language" since.

∽ 11 ∽

THE REST OF THE WAY

I had rooted all my dread in the hypothetical day when we would have to face the question of a feeding tube, when we would be forced to wrap our abstract opinions around our mother's locked up body and say No. Meanwhile, real days had unfurled into real months with their reassuring routine—lulling us into believing we could live forever in that Fifties fantasy, our precious mother at its center willing to love and be loved as she never had before.

The accident waiting to happen would only wait so long.

It was the same glitch that had brought on our father's death, and it made the feeding tube issue passé. On a Thursday in July when Chris was out of town on business, Mother choked on a spoonful of puree. After a fit of coughing that left her semi-conscious, she seemed to resume breathing adequately, so she was put to bed to await further developments.

By the next afternoon she was spiking a fever from pneumonia, but since Cathy and I were due the next morning for our visit, no one was called.

The head nurse waylaid us the minute we walked in from outside. She talked too fast for us to grasp details, but we understood that we were being alerted, prepared for a shock.

It was more a *déjà vu*. Mother's room had belonged briefly to our father: she was in the same bed he'd died in, cranked to the same angle, in the same light coma, the same gape of the lower jaw drawing the same labored breaths. The difference was the earrings—beautification by Patrice—large, pink pearlized clip-ons. They didn't seem to belong in the same universe, those earrings and the barely fleshed contours of her skull.

When we greeted her and touched her, noises of response tangled in her throat. Her eyelids twitched open then closed.

I was overcome by the fact that we were losing her. Some might have said she'd long been gone, but we'd found much to cling to, much to drape with old, old love stories, much to fill out in the image of our desires. All I could think was that I once adored her: I was six years old, or seven, when I used to gaze at her convinced she was the most unutterably beautiful woman on earth.

Cathy half-lay on the bed with her, one arm across the pillow, circling her head. "We love you so much, Mom," she whispered into her ear. "You don't need to hurry and you don't need to hold back. It'll just come and wrap you up like silk, and you can let yourself go."

168   Molly Best Tinsley

After a while, Chris arrived, and we explained what had happened. Then silent and hopeless, we witnessed her difficult breathing, the periodic jerking of her limbs. She kept raising a shaky clenched hand towards us, as if to hand something over. Her skin was hot, her pulse racing.

Chris had been saying good-bye to her since her speech stopped making sense to him. "She's gone," he'd report to us bluntly over the phone. "It's not Mom, that's it, she's not there." Maybe rushing the worst had allowed him to practice with the pain. But now he looked stricken. "I don't think I can go through this again," he said.

Just then, the staff doctor appeared in the doorway with his basset-hound eyes. The air turned brittle with mistrust. Cathy and I let Chris do the hand-shaking. I still bore a grudge over our father's treatment and couldn't even speak.

The doctor listened to her heart and repeated the story of what happened, which I was sure Mother did not need to hear. Chris mentioned our concerns about her comfort, the signs of stress and agitation, and the doctor proposed putting her on oxygen to ease her struggle for breath.

Then he suggested morphine suppositories to be sure that she experienced no discomfort. Chris agreed that was a good idea. For years I'd vainly preached at her, pleaded with her to accept roughness as part of life, to ride it out without resorting to pills. Dad had invoked will power. It was another issue passé. Dying was a roughness exempt from either approach. She should be allowed to take the edge off that.

If only the staff doctor hadn't swaggered so. If only his

need to control death had not been so strong that he thought he did. "I'll put her down for thirty milligrams every four hours," he said. "If I shot a dose like that straight into a vein, I'd wind up in jail." Then he added, "It'll be all over by tomorrow night max."

The next morning we found a pink rose in a vase on the tray at the foot of her bed. Patrice had scavenged it from some other bouquet. The pink earrings were in place. The flutters of movement in response to our voices died quickly into stillness. The sour smell of the nursing home, more concentrated in this room, grew stronger as we bent to kiss her cheeks.

Then there was nothing to do but sit. The oxygen unit pumped out its ominous two-beat rhythm, a pair of chords always mounting, sub-dominant to dominant, always promising the tonic resolution, never delivering.

A woman from housekeeping tiptoed in to check the wastebasket. She greeted Mother and told her she hoped she'd feel better soon. "She's the nicest lady," the housekeeper told us. "Such an elegant lady. Elegant even now."

I watched Mother's face for some sign of understanding. Wasn't that what she'd always wanted, all those selves of hers—the immigrant's daughter, the go-getter, the scholarship student, the subtly neglected wife, the depressive—what they'd never felt they deserved or could afford, to be found elegant and nice?

A little later, the rotund LPN waddled in and squished her broad belly against the foot of the bed. "Your mother's a good Christian," she announced. "I just know it."

Cathy and I exchanged a glance of mock horror. Should we tell her how Mother always scoffed at organized religion? How she and Dad used to argue about her flat-out refusal to attend church at his side? My college courses had turned up –*isms* to approximate the mélange of spiritual views I'd been dosed with as a child: Platonism, Transcendentalism, Buddhism, Aestheticism. But Christianity, particularly *good* Christianity, always got dismissed as empty show.

This nurse would have brushed aside that information anyway. "I can tell the good Christians," she continued. "They go through it so easy. They just tend to sit and play with their hands, and if you ask them what they're doing they say they're holding an angel." Her eyes took in the length of Mother's body—a skeleton under the bedclothes—and her face fell. "I can't stand not feeding them," she said.

Was this a reprimand? Would this nurse have preferred *heroic measures*? Intravenous nourishment spiked with antibiotics? For what purpose?

"But she's unable to eat," Cathy said firmly.

The nurse waggled her many chins. "With a child, I always think if you can get food into them, they'll get better."

"But this is the other end of the line," Cathy said as the woman left.

Marie wandered in, the first of several visits that day. On each we explained to her that our mother was dying, and on each Marie was shocked and saddened anew. She approached the bed and fumbled with the blanket, the pillows propping Mother's head, as if to re-tuck her in. She patted Mother's cheek, murmuring, "We've known Evelyn almost all her life." Then she backed away toward the door. "What sickness is it?" she asked, a *by-the-way*.

"Evelyn probably has Alzheimer's disease," we told her. "It's led to pneumonia."

"I don't know that one," said Marie.

When the shift changed, Barbara bustled in, greeting us gruffly as if nothing terrible were happening. The sight of the pink earrings seemed to bring her up short. She gave a loud *tsk-tsk* and shook her head. "What you need with these things anyway?" she asked Mother, then snap, snap, they were in the palm of her hand. She placed them in a little dish on the dresser, so that the next morning Patrice could find them and clip them back on.

A little later Chris arrived, intent on a mission. He took the looser of Mother's fists and wedged a leather pouch under her curled fingers. It was the same pouch with the blue stone that had received part of our father as he died. But now it also contained a second stone to receive our mother's spirit.

"If I know Mom," I said, "she'll be trying to squeeze into the one with Dad."

Chris seemed solider today. "If we were Native-Americans," he said, "this is what we'd be doing, sitting and waiting." We realized he was sharing an insight that had brought him some peace. His father's son, the torture of Mother's final months had been the helplessness of nothing left to try.

Chris also confessed that lying awake the night before, he had seen our father. And when Chris told him that he couldn't go through this with Mother, Dad had reassured him: "You can only do so much. I'm here. I'll get her the rest of the way."

Cathy and I changed our return flight to the following evening and signed up for one of the two rooms Evergreen reserved for visiting family. When we dragged upstairs at 10:30 that night, we turned the key and shoved open the door to a shriek of alarm, the terrified face of a stranger in the bed clutching the blanket to her chin.

We were not even surprised. We dragged back down to Pine where we enjoyed an exhausted chuckle with the night shift of nursing assistants. It was just one more bungle by the administration upstairs. Then refusing to let us help, they scrambled around to make up beds for us in two of Pine's empty rooms.

The next day brought no change.

Between the oxygen and the morphine, Mother's fever had come down, and her lowered pulse held steady around 80. She rested peacefully, in no hurry to have it "all be over."

Chris, Cathy, and I indulged in some manic glee over her defiance of the staff doctor's prediction. She'd been waiting all her life for someone to hook her up to round-the-clock euphoria. She wasn't about to give it up right away.

Cathy and I flew back to DC on Monday night to take care of families and jobs and returned to Durham on Wednesday morning to the same scene we'd left: the stilled, shrunken body on the bed, the endless, monotonous song of the oxygen, the smell of organic decay, which I had begun to discern everywhere. Maybe it's the smell of reality, the raw stuff every other smell grows out of and tries to escape. It clung to a wedge of focaccia, a cluster of grapes, cooked broccoli, lemons and grapefruit, all cheese. Whole veins of it opened when you tasted your own mouth in the morning, when a carton of milk started to turn, when you took off old shoes after a long day.

Meanwhile, time had stopped its advance, curved into a cycle of ritual duties, hushed speech, outbursts of tears.

Patrice or Barbara shifted Mother's position every few hours and changed her Depends, which she was still dampening, though she'd had no food nor fluids for a week.

Like the beak of a baby bird, her parched mouth sucked relief from the moistened swab covered with lemon-flavored petroleum jelly. Her body knew it was thirsty. I'd have given anything to be able to tip a glass of nice, cold water to those lips. Her head had stretched back further and further, as if trying to see the top of a cliff.

The dour, round LPN, the good Christian, returned to tell us that was a sign. So were her ears, which had rolled back close to her skull, and her feet, which had turned down like a dancer's *en pointe*.

Outside her room, life carried on. The staff members took their breaks in the kitchen where they found plenty of subjects for their hilarity to feed on.

Louise trotted in and looked suspicious when we told her our mother was dying: death, or talk of death, had been her province until now.

"I'm sorry to hear that," she snapped. "You have my con-
dolences." Then she trotted out.

When Marie entered, it was proudly to introduce her
daughter visiting from Vermont, who turned out to be the
woman we'd barged in on two nights ago in the guest room
upstairs. Once again Marie was surprised to find Mother in
such straits, and appropriately lowered her mood a notch.

Her daughter, a massage therapist, offered to smooth
Mother's energy. She drew her hands through the air above
Mother's limbs, from the pointed toes up to the strained neck
and down the arms, then the same motion in reverse. She told
us our mother was at peace—which certainly didn't refute
the evidence before us. Then Marie shuffled up to the head
of the bed and stroked Mother's forehead with her gnarled
hand, before she planted a kiss there. "Good-bye, Evelyn,"
she said. Then head bowed, she shuffled out.

When they were gone, Cathy and I tried to return to the
books we wouldn't remember a word of. But I kept thinking
of the body beside us, all the people with things to do for it,
things to say about it.

How many times had we watched Barbara strip it and flip
it, gently, proficiently, but without ceremony? She'd damp-
sponged the crepey flesh, the empty pouches of breasts, the
baggy buttocks, before she'd rewrap and rearrange the whole.

As considerate as she was, it was just a job for her, that
precious body, the first object I'd ever longed to possess, the
first object I'd had to learn to live without. The longing was
still there.

I smoothed the hair away from the brow, traced the curves of those flattened translucent ears, the bump that had returned to the bridge of her nose. Running my hand along the sheet, I touched one last time the shoulders, stiff arms, hands, the bent legs and bunched toes. I put my hand on her breastbone, which jutted like a helmet, and counted the heartbeats underneath.

Then I did what Marie's daughter did—I moved my hands through the air just above Mother's frame, up from the feet, the knees, to the waist, and then across the chest, where my hands started to tingle. There was a slight but unmistakable vibrancy, a fine turmoil.

Eyes closed to concentrate, I tried a different course, beginning along an arm, across the neck and face—all quiet—but again I came upon it, a subtle turbulence above her heart.

I called Cathy over to see if she could feel it. She said she did, though I sensed she was humoring me.

I stroked the air around our mother one more time, eyes shut, feeling the smooth flow under my hands break into something else. Like an estuary, where river current meets the tide of the sea.

It was Thursday evening. Her hands and feet were cold to the touch, a mottled blue, yet sweat beaded on her brow. She was breathing louder than the oxygen pump, and I was counting, 20-24 respirations per minute.

Cathy and I were both so numbed by almost a week of grief that we didn't notice at first that her eyes had opened. When we did notice, we scrambled to each side of her bed, insane hope crashing into the only possible conclusion, that this must be it.

We called to her, breathed her vocal breaths with her, murmuring *yes* on each exhale. We told her we were with her, we loved her, she was doing fine, we would miss her—surely she was beyond needing us, but we fell all over ourselves to reassure her—it was the arrogance of unbearable pain.

We caressed her arms, we kissed the top of her head which still somehow smelled sweet and maternal. With the sense of taking a great liberty, I placed my hand on the skin of her chest and counted a pulse of 100.

"I think I'd better get the nurse," I said, and Cathy looked at me as if I were crazy. *What could possibly go wrong?* That didn't stop me from rushing out to the central station and returning with the head nurse, a cold, business-like woman who talked without showing her teeth. By this time our mother's eyes had half-closed again, so there was nothing new as far as the nurse was concerned. She checked the patient's hands and feet, then left.

We pulled up chairs to each side of the bed and sat with our heads resting on her piled pillows. At the same moment we noticed that we were hearing silence. No breath.

Our heads snapped up, eyes met, and then Mother pulled in another loud draught of air.

After a minute of regular breathing, another long pause. It was as if she were testing her ability to go without air. As if she'd been building her courage to reach this point of letting go. She took a few breaths and then managed a longer pause, way too long, which she finally gave up, inhaling with a sob.

In that moment her eyes opened again and she looked right at Cathy, who thanked her and burst into tears. Then her lower jaw slowly lifted and she closed her mouth, which had been gaping open for weeks. We both saw the curve of a smile. We both saw her suddenly grow younger, lovelier, eyes clear and blue, face softened and filled out. She never took another breath.

Her heart was racing under my hand and I almost couldn't stand it. I wanted to do something. Wanted to run out of the room, screaming, *Help, help, someone call 911.* I had always been supposed to take care of our mother, keep her going, and now her pulse was tumbling, panicking, scared literally to death.

Cathy and I were stopped in our tears by a gasping noise: our mother's mouth opened and the lips retracted, the face contorted in a shocking grimace.

"My god," I whispered.

"What was that?" Cathy asked.

Who could guess?

The last cell shutting down?

The body's last-ditch objection to it all?

Excruciating pain? Orgasmic relief?

Something final.

I smoothed the lips back down over the teeth, the blue lids over the blank eyes.

She was clearly gone. She was not the body changing color, losing heat, tightening up before us. But I couldn't help

staring at the hospital gown that clothed it. Hoping to see it
rise with breath.

No.

Cathy clicked off the oxygen pump.

There was nothing more still than that room.

$\backsim$ 12 $\backsim$

EPILOGUE

In a dream I've dreamed since childhood, I get home from
school and home isn't there.

Sometimes the house is, but the front door opens on bare
rooms. I wander the neighborhood asking for news of my
family. Has my father been transferred? Did new orders arrive and no one remembered to tell me? People look at me
and shake their heads: *Sorry, we've never seen you before.*

Sometimes the street is gone too. I follow the proper
route right up to the last corner, but when I make that final
turn, instead of familiar residential contours, I find vacant
lots, maybe an airstrip or a factory.

The same longing I used to wake up with emptied whole
days after our father died. I saw him everywhere, disappearing
around corners, sitting behind the wheel of a car idling outside my window: the same imposing brow, the same glasses

with dark frames, the same forward thrust of the chin, which he recommended to me as the way to conceal an overbite.

It was worse after the death of our mother. I kept remembering things I needed to tell her, and that lost, left-behind feeling flared again. In the first months I sorted through saved letters, her notebooks, and those culled photographs, vowing to get them organized, mounted in albums. I vowed to get *myself* organized, to designate a *hoddy hole* or two, and generally to develop some consistent methods for the navigation of time and space, against the day when my own mind would grow loose as water. Too many thoughts already skipped across it like flat stones, sending up a spray, then sinking beyond retrieval.

Taking such initiatives helped me forget for a while that no matter how earnestly we inscribe them, our well-made stories implode. Characters relinquish character, the power to choose and act. Dialogue stops making sense. Poetic justice, like one of Mother's good ideas, tumbles right downstairs.

An appetite for happy endings will wear you out.

Some years ago now, I had my last fling with them. I threw a lot of less-than-beautiful things away and packed the rest for a preemptive move. One last time, from the East to the West, from the city to a small town in the mountains. I needed to do it myself, to cancel the chances of being stuck someday in a nursing home overlooking the sterile frenzy of the Capitol Beltway.

When I flew to Durham to say good-bye to Chris and his family, I couldn't not stop by Evergreen to see Barbara and

Patrice. I craved their quiet, their solidity, in a crazy, sloshing sea. The bite of salt in the air—I was missing that too.

I tried not to cling when I embraced them.

"Where's my picture?" Barbara asked right off, and I had to apologize. We'd promised to make her a copy of our mother's college yearbook portrait, which had sat on her dresser in Pine. I had to tell her that when Cathy took the frame apart and tried to separate the old photo from the cardboard behind it, everything crumbled.

As it happened, the day of my visit coincided with the First Annual Pine Fashion Show, to take place any minute in the Wandering Garden. The Fifties living room was packed with elderly models, all dressed up, some ambulatory, most in wheelchairs. Patrice resumed her scramble to apply make-up and back-comb hair.

None of the participants seemed to know what was going on except for Louise, whose face radiated an aloof smile. She was an old hand at fashion shows. "This was my major in college," she told me, pivoting one half-turn and then another, fist on canted hip.

The seven-year-old daughter of the charge nurse, similarly savvy and aloof in golden bathing suit and white boots, waited for her cue to twirl her baton.

An audience of relatives and other residents had assembled. The microphone was made to work. A Chihuahua in a tutu and tipsy tiara pranced the brick walk to lead things off.

Each model was announced, each outfit described in detail, as she or he marched slowly along the garden path or was pushed in a chair. Those of us who still possessed able minds and hands oohed and aahed and applauded vigorously. Insincerely. We were pretending, polishing that have-a-nice-day surface Cathy and I used to judge so severely. Now it seemed benign, an acknowledgment—*we are all in this together.*

The models took long minutes to cover the course, and I grew mildly bored. The Emcee's script lacked zip. It numbed with repetition. It needed a dash of our mother's spice, her poetry. So did I.

Someone's little grand-niece and nephew were getting the chance to wear their flower girl and ring bearer outfits a second time. They stepped solemnly to tinny, taped Lohengrin. The earnest blankness of their eyes promised that they would be good children, cute, adorable—they would play their appointed roles.

Young bodies coming, old bodies going: the fashion show crept on.

My gaze came to rest on the woman sitting serenely on the bench across from me. I realized I used to see her all the time during our parents' year of living independently—in the main dining room, in the cafeteria, on the walkways outdoors. Our mother always nudged me enviously and pointed her out—"That's the Yoga Teacher." The alternative woman, the authentic woman, growing old flexibly, confidently, someone to wish our mother were more like, a woman who could tell our father what to do.

The Yoga Teacher, with white bobbed hair and funny hat, its front brim bent up. Posture erect in comfortable dark blue pants and overshirt, her flat slippers not quite touching the ground, she appeared to be too deep in meditation to notice the models lurching and shuffling past.

Or the Chihuahua sniffing around her feet. Or me, when I thought I'd caught her eye. I smiled a warm greeting, ventured a wave. What she returned was a benignly oblivious stare.

Oh no, not her too, I realized, sinking into the old dismay. Beyond her loomed the mural's mountains, meadow, stream—clichés of tranquility.

Then an image flooded my mind's eye—Ray's good-sized lake a couple miles downstream, and it was sloshing everywhere, swallowing all our different paths. All at once, the burden of remembering lifted; loss seemed little more than a literary device. For a minute, I breathed the bright, pure simplicity of whatever it is that had carried us through.

WIE
Groveland, MA
22 June 2015
12:50 PM

Memoir from Fuze Publishing

The Gift of El Tio by Larry Buchanan and Karen Gans

When world-renowned geologist discovers an enormous deposit of silver beneath a remote Quechua village in Bolivia, he unknowingly fulfills a 450-year-old prophecy that promised a life of wealth for the villagers. Memoir.

Nobody Knows the Spanish I Speak by Mark Saunders

High-tech couple from Portland, Oregon, emigrates with large dog and ornery cat to San Miguel de Allende, in the middle of Mexico. Their well-intentioned cluelessness makes for mayhem and non-stop laughs. Humor/Memoir